A VETERINARIAN'S *LIFE*

and

A VETERINARIAN'S *WIFE*

by
Derry David Magee, DVM
and Gwendora Wilkes Magee, Ed.Spec.

"A Veterinarian's Life and A Veterinarian's Wife," by Derry David Magee, DVM and Gwendora Wilkes Magee, Ed.Spec. ISBN 978-1-62137-269-1 (Softcover).

Published 2013 by Virtualbookworm.com Publishing Inc., P.O. Box 9949, College Station, TX, 77842, US. ©2013, Derry David Magee, DVM and Gwendora Wilkes Magee, Ed.Spec. All rights reserved. No part of this publication may be reproduced, stored in a retrieval system, or transmitted in any form or by any means, electronic, mechanical, recording or otherwise, without the prior written permission of Derry David Magee, DVM and Gwendora Wilkes Magee, Ed.Spec.

Manufactured in the United States of America.

FOREWORD

Researching our family genealogies created a desire for us both to know more about our ancestors. We gathered information from cemeteries, libraries, family records, family notes, interviews, and Ancestry.com which motivated us to write our autobiographies. This book includes our family genealogies and our stories as a veterinarian and a veterinarian's wife.

THANKS

There are many people to thank but, first of all, that would be our parents, Marvin and Mary Magee and Earl and Willie Wilkes for their constant support, and Dr. Carl Keller who was my partner in veterinary medicine in Kentwood for 25 years. Our practice partnership was the oldest in the state of Louisiana for a long time. We also want to thank Dr. Bill Moyer, Department Head of the Large Animal Medicine and Surgery at Texas A&M University, for his support during my seventeen years associated with this Department. A special thanks to Nancy Linger for her friendship and technology support. This book is our effort to tell our family "who we are and how we got to be that."

DEDICATION

This book is dedicated to our daughter, Juanita Elaine Magee Johnson and husband, Steven Winslow Johnson, who have given us much joy in our lives. We are very proud of their successes in pursuing their careers and raising their three children. We are very blessed to have three grandchildren: Jennifer, Bill, and Ross Johnson and two great-grandchildren, Mia Mckenzie and William Chase Johnson whose mother, Kellye, is a great addition to our family.

A Veterinarian's *Life*

Growing Up in New Orleans, Louisiana

I WAS BORN AT 3021 Lafitte Avenue in New Orleans, Louisiana, on July 5, 1934. My father was Marvin Mangum Magee, son of Zora Easterling and Derry David Magee. His paternal grandmother was Eugenia Elizabeth Mangum. My mother was Mary Alline Bridges, daughter of Juanita Rivers Bankston Bridges and Cannon Wilson Bridges.

Lafitte Avenue is parallel to Bayou St. John, which connects the New Orleans East pumping station and Lake Pontchartrain. I have trouble documenting the existence of Lafitte Street, but I know that Bayou St. John was just across the street from our house. We lived in a "shotgun" house that set on piers. I spent a lot of time playing with my horses and wagons under the house and would hide them on floor joists when company came. I still have these horses and wagons in a case upstairs here at 9265 Brookwater Circle, College Station, Texas 77845. Actually, before I was walking, Mother and Daddy took me to the City Park Pony Ride. Daddy would tie me on the pony with his belt, and I would ride around the little corral for as long as they would remain. When they removed me from the pony, I cried myself to sleep. This was the early beginning of my fascination with animals.

I remember one young friend, Henry Zimmerman, who on occasion would visit to play. The memory is of Henry going to mother and saying in his New Orleans accent, "Mrs. Magee, Derry hit me on my yed." Now, why this happened, I do not remember. I had a collie dog that watched over us, as well as, played with us. I don't remember anything special about this dog, but she was the first in a long line of collie dogs that we had through the years.

Sometime around my fifth birthday, my family moved to 411 Hullen Street, Metairie, LA, in Jefferson Parish. When compared to the Lafitte Street house, this house was a mansion. There was a large yard and a chicken yard in back of the house. While caring for the chickens in this yard, I learned to hate chickens. In this yard, was a very large willow tree. Friends and relatives who visited us would climb into the tree and jump from limb to limb. Of course, this finally caused a limb to break and fall on the chicken yard fence. My daddy's logic was that anything that happened on our premises was my fault, regardless of who was actually at fault. This resulted in my receiving a "belting" from my Daddy.

During this growing-up period of my life, Daddy was a Greyhound bus driver. Most of the time, he was gone one day and back at home the next day. In our yard, was a type of grass that put out long, upright seed heads. It was my job to use a hoe and chop the seed heads off, even though the next day the grass had regenerated another seed head. About this time in our history, the United States was at war in World War ll. The family motto in response to local economic conditions was: "Eat it up, wear it out, Make it do or do without!" (It still is to this day). Everyone was encouraged to grow a "victory garden." Next to our house was a vacant lot approximately one and one/half acre in size. My parents received permission to use this lot for a "victory garden." With this garden in active use, I was allowed to help with the weeding, cultivating, and harvesting of the produce. Mother and Grandmother Juanita Rivers Bridges preserved an unbelievable amount of vegetables from this garden.

I started school while living on Hullen street. I attended Ella Dolhonde Elementary School at 219 Severn Avenue, which intercepted Metairie Road in Jefferson Parish. I was an avid reader and enjoyed going to school. I walked to school which was about six blocks from our house. I attended Ella Dolhonde until we moved to the Line Creek Community in Tangipahoa Parish.

My parents bought a home in Metairie on Johnson Street, which intersects Severn Avenue. The house was located west of the Ella Dolhonde School. This house was located several houses from the Faller's home where I made the acquaintance of Carlton Faller and his sisters. (Dr. Carlton Faller has been a medical doctor in Kentwood, La. for over 50 years where he and Janice raised four children: Julie, Susan, Carlton, Jr. and John.) Also, at this Metairie address, I learned to care for broilers (young chickens), as well as, learned how to process the broilers for the market. I learned to hang the broilers up by their feet and use a sharp pointed knife to pith them. This caused the feathers to be loosened and made the broiler easier to clean for the house and market. Also at this house, Daddy would tell me not to leave to go around the street corner. Being somewhat obstinate, I would leave as soon as he went back into the house. When he realized that I was gone, he immediately set out to find me, and when he found me, I got a lesson in obedience. However, these lessons did not help resulting in my receiving many whippings.

After a period of time, we moved back to 411 Hullen Street to a house which was across the street from our original Hullen Street home. Again, this house was larger than either of the two previous homes. We had to install new plumbing in this house; therefore, I spent a lot of time under the house helping Daddy with the pipes. At this house, I made the acquaintance of a dear friend named Willy. Willy was a black male goat that got to be a member of the family. Daddy took the tongue off a red wagon and fixed shafts to harness the goat to the wagon. The neighborhood friends and I spent many happy times with Willy, pulling the wagon up and down the side walk. At times, Willy would rebel and decide not to cooperate. During these times, I used a sharp pointed stick to persuade him to cooperate. As he got older, he learned to open the kitchen door when the door was not locked. He would come into the kitchen and jump on the eating table, which resulted in a noisy confrontation with mother. He also had an affinity for the front porch, which made it necessary to sweep the porch clean after he slept on it. Eventually, we took him to Uncle Galloway Magee's farm in Collins, Mississippi. Of course, a goat raised on the streets of Jefferson Parish was not educated in the ways to survive in the country. The Leif River flooded, and Willy drowned in the flood. In addition to all of the escapades with Willy, I would tease my sister, Mary Jane, by telling her that Willy was coming to get her, and sometimes antagonizing her by calling her, "Willy, Willy, Willy" which never failed to get the appropriate response.

Baptist Preacher's Son

DADDY DROVE NEW ORLEANS street cars and public buses when we lived in New Orleans and later in Metairie. When I was twelve years old, he heard the prompting of the Holy Spirit calling him to surrender to preach. He used the Biblical principle, called "putting out a fleece." (see Gideon in Judges 6:38-40) He and mother were in the real estate business during this time. He asked that they make and save enough money to support the family during his seminary training. They made approximately $10,000.00 during that year. Thus, his fleece was answered. By that day's standards, that amount of money was a very large sum. As well as I can remember, he was thirty six years old at that time. He had changed jobs and was driving for the Greyhound Bus Company. He had received an invitation to go to Terry's Creek Baptist Church, Amite County, Mississippi to supply for that church for one Sunday. He had made arrangements for a substitute driver for that Sunday. When he went into the supervisor's office to tell him that he would be asking a substitute to take his run on the next Sunday, the supervisor told him that it was not possible for him to do this. He removed his badge and gave it to the supervisor. He told the supervisor that he was resigning his driver position. He left his job to preach one sermon. I have always admired his commitment to his calling. How many of us would stand up for what we felt was the right thing to do? He had a wife and two children at home. As far as I know, he never missed preaching on Sunday for the rest of his life.

A delegation from Line Creek Baptist Church (northern Tangipahoa Parish, Louisiana) was at the Terry's Creek Baptist Church that Sunday and asked that he preach at their church the next Sunday. He agreed to preach for them and was invited back for several Sundays. The church voted to call him to be their pastor, and he agreed to serve. He was the Line Creek Baptist Church pastor for three years (1946 to 1949). The family moved from New Orleans (Metairie) to the Line Creek community. Because the church had no parsonage, we moved to a small house in Mississippi. The house had electricity but no running water and no indoor toilet facilities. We had to climb through a barbed wire fence to get to the outhouse. When you wanted water, you primed the pump with water left at the pump. You had to move the handle of the pump up and down to cause the water to flow to the top of the well. After a short time, a gasoline engine was hooked to the well pump allowing you to start the engine that pumped the water. All the wash water and drinking water was secured in this fashion. There was no hot water other than that heated on the stove. Thank goodness we had a propane stove, so that we did not have to chop wood to heat the water. The house had two bedrooms and a kitchen. My bedroom wall had cracks in it. It snowed our first winter there. You can imagine how surprised I was to wake up the next morning with snow piled up that had sifted through the wall cracks. On one occasion, an unwanted guest came into the bedroom making itself at home in one of the drawers in the chest of drawers. I don't remember what species of snake this one was, and it does not matter, because I do not like snakes, and this one was killed. Later the church purchased a house across the road from the church that was remodeled into more comfortable living quarters.

My First Christmas in the Country

MY FIRST CHRISTMAS AT the Mississippi house is the most memorable, and the best Christmas a 12 year-old could ever have. For years, when asked what I would like for Christmas, I would ask for a horse. "If you can't have a horse, what else would you like?" My answer was always the same. "If I can't have a horse, I don't want anything." Well, to my surprise! I got a small bay mare (mustang) with black mane and tail. I named her Molly. Someone had reworked an old saddle for me. Although it had several shades of leather in the reworked areas, it was in very good shape. Believe me! This was the best Christmas for which a boy could ask.

Experiences with Friends on Line Creek

JESSIE DEAN HAD A black and white pinto gelding named "Go." We would get together and ride all through the woods around our area. We would sometimes meet at Lucas Simmons farm just in the edge of Mississippi. This farm had a long flat bottom of land which we would race over. My little mare only lost one race over this bottom. This was when she was pregnant. We usually rode bare back, Indian style. In the pasture next to our house was a terrace row that curved the length of the pasture. The mare was trained to walk to the far end of the terrace, and when she walked over the terrace she would take off running like a race horse coming out of the starting gate on a race track. My first cousin wanted to ride on one of his visits from New Orleans. I very carefully instructed him to walk to the terrace and cross over it. Of course, when the mare crossed over the terrace, she launched into full stride. The cousin was left on the ground at the end of the terrace.

The new parsonage was across the road from the Line Creek church and north of the Line Creek Cemetery. A gravel road ran between the parsonage property and the cemetery. This road branched off the main Line Creek road and continued along the edge of the cemetery. It was a common practice for dairy farmers to travel their herd down one of these roads, across the Line Creek and on to a pasture. In the afternoon, the farmer would go and get his dairy cattle and walk them over the road back home for milking. Mr. Oris Lea followed this route with his small herd of jersey milk cows. One afternoon we boys found a newly dug grave just adjacent to the road. We had a great idea for some fun. We got into the grave and waited for Oris to drive his cows home. When the cows were directly adjacent to the freshly dug

8

grave site, we began to moan and bellow as loud as we could. The cows scattered similar to a covey of quail flying off the ground. Oris seemed to be very irritated by this prank and proceeded to try to gather his cows back together, but they were reluctant to go back by the grave. He finally got them home, and then he proceeded to come to our house and complain to the preacher about his son and friends. Of course, I got the tar beat out of me, but it was worth the whipping to remember how those cows scattered. I can still see them in my mind to this day!

Line Creek—the Center of Recreation and Baptistries for Local Churches

LINE CREEK IS A SMALL, clear, spring fed stream of water. The water is very cold. The creek runs immediately behind the church. Across the road is the Line Creek swim hole. Sacks of sand were laid at the head of the water coming down the creek at the upper end of the swimming hole. As the water ran over the sand bags, it had a tendency to wash the bottom of the swimming hole clean and keep it from filling in with sediment and other trash. From time to time, we would swim the horses out into the swimming hole, and their swimming would stir the bottom and cause any debris deposited by the current to wash off downstream. This swimming hole also served as a baptismal pool for the local churches. As near as I can remember, my sister Mary Jane was baptized in the Creek and seems to have a vivid memory of how cold the water was in the Creek.

The Creek was surrounded on both sides of the banks by dense hardwood and pine trees. This was perfect woods for hunting squirrel and rabbit. I was not that dead-eye shot that hit these small creatures in the eye with the rifle bullet and really did not diminish their population to any great extent. On one of these excursions, I was a little farther than usual down the side of the creek. I heard something singing through the tree tops. The next time I heard the noise, it was a little closer. I realized that these were warning shots and not really meant to actually hit me but letting me know that I was too close to one of the whiskey stills, and it was time to turn around and get back out of that general location.

There were several stills that operated down the creek. The area was perfect for making whiskey. The pots could be heated with the vapor running down cooling tubes in the creek where the vapor condensed into white lightening. The only road that crossed the creek was adjacent to the Line Creek church. Much further down, the creek was crossed by Highway 51. Between these two crossings were several miles of dense woods with only an occasional foot path going down to the creek —ideal territory for making whiskey. One prominent citizen had wooden barrels of whiskey buried in his front yard. Locals who imbibed said that the man sold the best that could be purchased.

Line Creek—a "Closely Knit" Community

THE LINE CREEK COMMUNITY is located on the Mississippi-Louisiana state line north of Kentwood, La. in Tangipahoa Parish, one of the Florida Parishes with the Line Creek forming the boundary between these two states. Highway 1053 turns off Highway 51 just north of Kentwood and goes to the state line and forms the Line Creek Community. Line Creek community was composed of the Line Creek Baptist Church, Line Creek Cemetery, and surrounding farms in Louisiana and Amite County, Mississippi. The children of this community attended school in the town of Kentwood where the farmers shopped for groceries, clothing, animal feed, lumber, hardware, and attended movies.

Kentwood is the most northernmost town in Tangipahoa Parish. The name of the town does not stem from the earliest settlers who came there in the first decade of the nineteenth century, among them the Amackers and the Tates. Kentwood honors, instead, Amos Kent (1811-1906) who came to the area about 50 years later. Kent, originally of Chester, New Hampshire, sailed to New Orleans, walked to Baton Rouge, moved to Greensburg, and eventually settled in the vicinity of Kentwood. At this time, the New Orleans, Jackson and Great Northern Railroad was being constructed through the region, and Kent established a lumber mill and brick plant on the railroad just south of where the town was to develop.

On Line Creek Road, Highway 1053, northwest of his mills, Kent built his home, Oak Hill. Here he lived happily with his wife, the former Susan Fluker, and 12 children. This home is approximately one mile from the home that we built in 1978 on land that was part of the Dr. Ellis Estate on Line Creek road.

Because I spent three enjoyable years growing up in the Kentwood-Line Creek area, we chose to build our home on Line Creek Road. We named our home Juanwood after our daughter Juanita and the dogwood trees on the land.

The inhabitants of this Line Creek community were hard-working farmers who lived in this parish known as "Bloody Tangipahoa."Tangipahoa Parish is known for its violent history due to racial, ethnic, and family conflicts throughout the Parish. As a result of this reputation, while passenger trains were traveling down the railroad, the conductor instructed the passengers to duck behind the seats until the train had passed through the Village of Tangipahoa, just five miles south of Kentwood and ten miles south of the state line.

Violence—Contributed to "Bloody Tangipahoa"

Some families in the Line Creek community contributed to the reputation of "Bloody Tangipahoa" as their families feuded and used violence to try to solve their conflicts. Here are a few of the stories that I remember while living in this community where my father was pastor at the Line Creek Baptist Church for three years.

One example of settling a conflict through violence was the Saul incident. One day, as Saul was plowing in his corn field, Isaac's son climbed a tree near the field and shot Saul, wounding him in the leg. This incident began a feud between the two families.

Peter, a cousin of Saul and a relative of many in the community, was shot by Timothy causing Peter to lose an arm. On a separate occasion, Peter and Benjamin were traveling from Kentwood in a vehicle. As they came over the crest of the hill, they saw Saul waiting for them. Peter and Benjamin stopped at the crest of the hill. Peter got out of the vehicle and had Benjamin turn around and go back toward Kentwood. Peter walked down the hill and when he came close to Saul, Saul was so enraged that he killed his cousin Peter. At Peter's wake, Timothy walked up to the coffin and announced, "You S.O.B., if I had known that you were not dead when I shot off your arm, you would not be a corpse tonight."

One evening, I was attending a Line Creek Baptist Church Sunday School social at a home along with Tom. I received a telephone call me to bring Tom home. When we arrived at his house, his father lay dead in the gate to the house. His father had been shot through the throat, destroying both carotid arteries. His mother was sitting on the front porch of their house when the Coroner arrived. Questions began to arise about Paul's assailant. Directly in front of the yard gate was a tree with a fork about four feet from the ground. Two empty shot gun shells were found at the base of the tree.

There were and still remain questions as to who murdered Paul. The bloodhounds were brought from the Angola Penitentiary. King was an Angola inmate who handled the bloodhounds. King and the deputies followed the bloodhounds down the hill. They crossed to the east side of Line Creek behind the Line Creek Baptist Church where they crossed over to the west side of the creek. As they crossed to the west side of the creek, a very violent rain storm occurred stopping the ability of the bloodhounds to track any farther. Consequently, the question of who shot Paul has never been answered.

14

During the three years that my father, Rev. Marvin M. Magee, pastored the Line Creek Baptist Church, he preached 22 funerals, 18 of which were violent deaths. While the people of this community were kind and considerate, at times, they settled their differences by violent means. These people loved my family and showed their affection and appreciation by showering us with bountiful supplies of vegetables from their gardens.

On the occasion of King's release from Angola, he met his son in Kentwood, two blocks from the Kentwood High School. They talked while in King's vehicle. For some unknown reason, King shot and killed his son.

Many years later, as I was practicing veterinary medicine in the Kentwood area, one of my clients operated a dairy farm on the east bank of the Tangipahoa River south of the town of Tangipahoa, La. This farmer thought that an employee was flirting with his wife and went down to the dairy barn to confront the employee.

The employee responded by saying that he was going home to get his gun. When the employee returned to the farm, the owner was waiting in the dairy barn. As the employee was exiting his vehicle, holding his gun, the owner stepped out of the barn and began shooting the man and killed him on the spot. Of course, this ruled self-defense by the Sheriff and Grand Jury.

A short time after this incident, I received a call to go to the farmer's dairy farm to treat a cow. The employees at my veterinary clinic asked if I were going to the farm to treat the cow. I replied, "I am afraid to go, and I am also afraid not to go." So, I went and was received by the farmer as if nothing had ever happened. I treated his cow and returned to the office.

Later, this farmer's son began dairying with his dad. The son had purchased 20 cows financed by the Farmers Home Administration (FHA). Several years later, the FHA wanted an inventory of the cattle that they had financed. The farmer told them that they had died. The FHA needed a statement to that effect. I told the farmer that we would have to find 20 skeletons before I could verify his statement. He said, "Okay, come to the farm." He took me down to the river swamp, and sure enough, we counted over 20 skeletons. I had no proof that these skeletons were from the financed cows, but we had counted 20 skeletons.

No one was ever charged for the murders of these incidents that I have recorded.

Road to Veterinary Medicine

MY EARLIEST MEMORY IS that I wanted to be a veterinarian. There was never any thought of any other occupation or profession. While living at Line Creek community, daddy took me aside and told me that he and mother were not going to be financially able to send me to college. If I went to college, I would have to have to help make my way. I had started raising heifer calves at this time. The people living in the Line Creek community were very special. Dempsey Newman, S.E. Dean and Lucas Simmons were the people who supplied me with heifer calves. They and others generously gave me dairy type heifers in return for collie puppies. Lucas Simmons allowed me to keep my cows at his farm. They were bred to a Brahman bull, and all ten had calves.

Lucas raised mules. I would help him break the mules to work by driving them hitched to a log. He also raised calves. He would have as many as 8 to 12 calves on one cow. The youngest calves were allowed to nurse for a short time. They were then removed and four more calves would be allowed to nurse. These would then be removed and older calves were allowed to finish nursing. When it was time to de-worm and vaccinate the calves, Lucas would build a pine log corral with a pine sapling chute exiting off the corral. I often helped him take care of the young cattle. He used an old time remedy to de-worm the cattle; Blue Stone (copper sulfate) and Black Leaf 40 (nicotine). This mixture was actually very effective against round worms; ascarids, strongyles and tapeworms. When the cattle would exit the chute, urinate, and then lie down, you knew that the dose was just right. They were vaccinated against "black leg" (*Clostridium chauvoei, and other species of Clostridium)*

Our Family Move Brought New Opportunites to My Journey

WE MOVED TO MT. HERMON when daddy was called to pastor the Mt. Hermon Baptist Church. This was sometime in the late fall of 1946. There I was able to lease a 120 acre farm from Mr. Seth Alford. This farm had a creek flowing through it and was on the banks of Silver Creek. It is located about 3 miles from the Mt. Hermon Church parsonage. I would ride my bay mare to and from the farm twice a day —each morning before school and again after school.

Seth had a pair of mules that went with the lease of the farm. I used these mules to plow and plant winter pasture, rye grass, oats and crimson clover. One of the mules was named Sam. If you were plowing with him as a single animal hitched to the plow, you had to watch his ears. If he began to work his ears forward and back, you had better stop and let him settle down, because if you did not stop plowing, he would run away taking the plow with him and tearing up untold amounts of the crop. On one occasion, I was plowing with a "Georgia stock" which is a beam with a foot attached which serves as a stock with which the plow points are attached. On this occasion, I decided to teach Sam a lesson. When he started to wiggle his ears, I jammed the stock into the dirt to the level of the beam. This should surely stop him! Much to my surprise, he bunched his hind quarters and took off breaking the beam off the stock. He proceeded to ruin at least an acre of corn with the beam bouncing and swinging around behind him. I had borrowed the Georgia stock from Mr. Alonso Alford. I had to completely rebuild the plow before taking it back to Mr. Alford.

Through the three years on this farm, my dairy herd grew from 10 cows to 30 cows. Seth Alford's son helped me milk. We milked these 30 cows twice a day by hand. The milk from the heifers was strained and poured over an ice bank cooler and then into ten gallon cans. Mr. Earl Wilkes (my future father-in law) picked up the cans of milk and transported them to Mt. Hermon. At the receiving station, the empty cans were rinsed and washed. Mr. Earl would return the cans and set them off by the driveway. The cans and all the buckets were washed again and disinfected before the next milking was started.

A Disastrous Event in My Dairy

A TRAGEDY DEVELOPED DURING this episode of my life. Some of the cows contracted Brucellosis and 14 of the pregnant cows aborted their calves. This disease is transmissible to humans, causing those coming in contact to develop undulant fever. I was advised that all of the herd should be vaccinated with a vaccine to stop them from aborting. This was done, and the rest of the herd that was pregnant aborted as a result of being vaccinated with a live vaccine. The cows were branded with a "V" on their right jaw to identify that they had received this live vaccine. This would later become an issue when it was time to sell the farm.

My Daddy thought that in order to plant a crop the land had to be plowed and then put into rows to plant the crop. In February, I would flat break the corn ground by plowing with the team of mules pulling a 14 inch turning plow. Most farmers used a 7 inch turning plow to flat break their fields, but using the larger turning plow allowed for covering more ground and also plowing deeper. The rows were "laid off" using a middle buster. After the corn was planted and began to grow, a "Georgia stock" with a sweep and a heel sweep was used to sweep out the middle of the rows.

In the fall, oats, rye grass, and clover were planted. Oats were plowed into dirt with a 7 inch turning plow. Rye grass and clover were broadcast by hand. The field was leveled using a section harrow. Crops were used during the winter for grazing, and in the early spring, these crops would be harvested for hay.

Every Saturday, the corn and hay needed for the next week's cow feed would be hauled to town and crushed. As the crushed feed came out of the hammer mill, a light spray of molasses was applied. A 100 bag of cottonseed meal was purchased, and the cottonseed meal and crushed corn and hay were hauled back to the farm to be mixed together using a shovel. This feed mixture would be fed to the cows using a 25 pound size bucket full of feed for them to eat while being milked.

I had originally leased the farm, but later bought the farm and mules from Mr. Alford. Once I owned the farm, Dad helped me buy a John Deere Tractor and implements to plant the crops. Boy! I was in "high cotton" to borrow a saying that meant I was really progressing. My senior year the crops were planted using the tractor.

Met My Wife and Life Partner at Mt. Hermon High

I NEED TO DIGRESS at this point. While attending school at Mt Hermon High School, I was on the basketball team. In that small school, physical education was scheduled during the regular school time and not after the school day ended. This enabled me to practice basketball and also milk my cows, before school and after school. There was a corn field behind the schoolyard. Sometime after starting Mt. Hermon High School, I walked into the cafeteria and there sitting at one of the tables was the most beautiful young lady dressed in blue denim jeans, wearing a blue denim long sleeve shirt and a red bandana handkerchief tied around her neck. My! Oh! My! Who was this beautiful young lady? As fate happens, or in the fullness of God's timing, she was Gwendora Wilkes, second daughter of Mr. Earl Wilkes and Mrs. Willie Wilkes, who would later become my wife. At the time of this writing, we will have been married 60 years. On that fateful day, she had come into the cafeteria to eat lunch while plowing her dad's corn crop planted in Mr. Fleet Miller's field behind the school yard. She often did tractor work with and for her dad.

When it was time to "lay by the corn" during my senior year at Mt. Hermon, I got sick and could not finish my crop. By this time, Gwendora and I were dating and had become very close to each other. She borrowed her dad's tractor and came to the Alford farm. There she proceeded to finish plowing out my corn, or as the term is used to "lay by the crop."

While attending Mt. Hermon high school, I was enrolled in the Future Farmers of America Chapter. My FFA project was the dairy farm. Very detailed records were kept on income and

22

expenses of the farm with these records being turned into the state and later the national FFA organization. On the foundation of these dairy farm records, I began to progress through the levels of achievement. I eventually became the second person in the State of Louisiana to achieve the designation of "American Farmer" which is a national title. James Lee Holiday was the first to receive this award just a few years ahead of me. My best friend, Quinlon McElveen, who later became a brother-in-law by marrying Bobbie Earl, Dora's sister, also attained the "American Farmer" degree.

At the time of my graduation, (Valedictorian 1952 graduating class, GPR 4.0), my parents and I had to decide what to do with the farm. We thought of selling the cattle and then the farm, only to learn that the cattle had been adult vaccinated for brucellosis. This meant that the cattle could only leave the premises to go to slaughter. This was not an acceptable solution. Daddy and mother decided that they would continue to operate the farm. Of course sister, Mary Jane, also had to help which did not make her happy. To their credit, by this time, we had a mechanical milking system (Surge bucket) and a John Deere H tractor. This made the operation of the farm much easier than it had been when mule power handled the plowing and hand milking took care of producing the milk. It was agreed that the family would send me $100.00 per month while I was in college as a payment for the farm enterprise.

An article appeared in the local newspaper, *The Era Leader*, stating that in the ordinary progression of time a son would inherit property from the father. However, on this occasion, the father inherited a farm from his son. My family only operated the farm for a short period of time. A Korean War veteran was able to obtain financing to buy the farm and the cows. They continued to send me my monthly stipend all the way through veterinary school.

Pre-veterinary Medicine at Louisiana State University

DURING MY FIRST SEMESTER attending LSU, I married the love of my life who has been a faithful companion through these 57+ years. (More about our story later.) At the end of my freshmen year at LSU, I was fortunate to have the highest GPA of all the freshmen class in agriculture which qualified me for a $1,000.00 yearly scholarship given by the Borden Company. By this time, our daughter Juanita was born so the scholarship money for the next semester was greatly appreciated by Dora and me.

We shared a bathroom in a two family apartment on West Roosevelt Street in Baton Rouge, while I attended LSU. This house was two houses down from the railroad track which caused our silverware on the table to rattle when the trains passed by. On one occasion, the wife in the apartment in the front of the house complained loudly about the cleanliness of the shared bathroom. I told Dora that was fine! "From now own just let her clean the toilet."

At the end of my freshmen year at LSU 1952-53, Dora and I moved back to Mt. Hermon for the summer where I worked with Pearly Conerly on Mr. T. H. Cutrer's dairy farm. Juanita Elaine Magee was born at Walthall County Hospital in Tylertown, Miss. on May 3, 1953. Shortly after Nita was born, we moved into a large front bedroom apartment with a kitchen and bath in the beautiful historic home of Mr. and Mrs. Fleet Miller at Mt. Hermon.

In September of 1953, we moved back to the house on West Roosevelt St. in Baton Rouge, La. this time in the two-room front apartment. I was hired by the LSU Veterinary Science Department to raise calves at the Anaplasmosis Research Barn. The Research Barn was across the railroad track from the LSU main campus. I arose early and walked down the railroad track to the Research Barn where I raised orphan bull calves for the department. I changed clothes at the barn and walked to classes on campus. In the afternoon after classes, I walked back to the barn, tended to the calves, and walked back up the railroad track to our apartment.

At the Research Barn, we had a very large red white-face cow that was half holstein. We raised 12 calves at the time on this cow. We let four of the youngest calves nurse for four minutes, then we would let four of the next oldest calves nurse for four minutes, and followed up with the four oldest calves to finish nursing. We followed this procedure in the mornings and in the afternoons. We nursed the oldest calves until they were two months old. At that time they were weaned and finished on grain and hay. When these oldest calves were weaned, four young calves were acquired and started nursing as the youngest group at this time. After the calves were weaned, their spleens were surgically removed. This was done so that they could be used in various fashions in the Anaplasmosis Research. In May of 1954, we moved back to Mt. Hermon where we lived in the three bedroom house on the Magee dairy farm.

Veterinary Medical Education at Texas A&M College

IN THE FALL OF 1954, I moved to College Station, TX where I began my freshmen year at Texas A&M College of Veterinary Medicine. Dean W. W. Armistead greeted me and his secretary made telephone calls to help me find lodging. As soon as I located the "chicken coop" at the termination of Cooner St. in College Station for $18.00 a month, our families moved Dora and Nita to College Station in "Mr. Earl's" milk truck. The house contained three rooms: an enclosed front porch for the small living area and a bedroom so small that we had to jump across the bed to get to the other side. Behind these two rooms was another room that contained the bathroom, a kitchen and eating area with a corner for Nita's baby bed. On one occasion, Dora was getting ready to get into bed when a scorpion was hiding under the bed spread. It stung her when she placed her foot under the spread as she jumped into the bed. It was very common to find a scorpion in the bathtub.

Again, I had to depend on walking to get to class. I walked from the end of Cooner to the Mark Francis Building on the Texas A&M College campus in the morning and back home in the afternoon. Dora and Nita rode to the grocery store with neighbors, Mr. and Mrs. Blackie Gossett. We also rode to Calvary Baptist Church each Sunday with the Gossetts.

Received Family and Church Support

IN THE SPRING OF 1955, Dora began to bleed and was hospitalized for three days in Bryan, TX. Dora was to be discharged, but I did not have the money to pay the hospital charges. Calvary Baptist Church members took up an offering to pay the $50.00 to the hospital for the discharge.

Dora's father and my father drove to College Station to take Dora and Nita back to Louisiana. Dora and I had to give up the little house (chicken coop) on the end of Cooner Street. I moved into the civilian dorm on the University campus and ate meals in Sebisa, the civilian dining hall. Meals were served family style with about eight students to a table. Many of the students did not like the cooking at the Sebisa dining hall. I loved it. I usually got to eat several servings of the main course plus desert because some at my table would sit down and then decide to go to town and get something to eat. "A country boy will survive."

The Bryan doctors and the doctors at Walthall County Hospital in Tylertown, Miss. thought that Dora was pregnant, but she was not. She had a hydatid mole in the uterus which later became *Chorionepithelioma,* which is a malignant cancer. She began to pass parts of the cancer through the uterus, and an emergency hysterectomy had to be performed.

Not having a vehicle, I hitched-hiked to Tylertown, Miss. (480 miles) to be there for Dora's surgery. It was dark when I arrived in Elton, La., a small town with little traffic. It took several hours for me to catch a ride on to Baton Rouge. I remained with Dora for a few days before hitch-hiking back to College Station. The ride put me out at the foot of the Mississippi River Bridge at Baton Rouge well after dark. When a car pulled up and stopped, the driver asked me if I could drive. I told him,

"Yes sir, I can." It turned out that this driver was a driller for an oil drilling rig and had been up for close to 36 hours with no sleep. I got into the car and began driving. He immediately went to sleep. Very early the next morning, we arrived in Beaumont. He asked me if I were hungry. Of course, I was always hungry. He bought my breakfast, gave me $10.00, and wished me well on my way to College Station. During that era, college students frequently hitched rides to and from school. Hitch-hiking would not be a safe way to travel today.

Worked During Summer Break

DURING THE SUMMER OF 1955 while Dora was recuperating from surgery at her parents' home, I got a job working for G.T. Patterson at the Mandeville Causeway Bridge construction site. The bridge roadway sections were poured five sections at the time. From one end of the five sections to the opposite end were groups of steel cable. A large amount of pressure was applied to the cable. Then concrete was poured to form the road sections containing the stressed cable. After the concrete had set and aged for several days, we cut the cable between the sections using an acetylene torch. Steel cables were wound around a drum and welded with the exception of four or five wraps on each end which had to be welded by hand. The welded cage was removed from the drum and placed in a form where it became steel reinforcing for the 18 foot sections of piling.

Shortly after I started working for Mr. Patterson, he formed a night crew under the supervision of his brother. There were four college boys plus Mr. Patterson's two sons who set a record for the most production work done on this construction yard.

About six weeks into the summer, my father-in-law, Earl Wilkes, had a heart attack—a coronary thrombosis. He picked up cans of milk from various farms and delivered them to Borden receiving station in Kentwood, LA. Because of this illness, he was unable to continue picking up the cans of milk. I filled in for him driving the truck and picking up the milk until I returned to Texas A&M. To put this into perspective, I picked up the cans of milk each morning and drove to Mr. Patterson's construction site in Mandeville to work the night shift. A full ten-gallon can of milk weighs 96 pounds. The door to the bed of the truck was chest high. There is a definite art to swinging the cans from the

29

ground and setting them in the bed of the truck. There were shelves in the bed of the milk truck that held the cans of milk with holes to hold them in place on the shelves. At the Borden receiving plant, each farmer's milk was sent from the truck into the plant on a track of rollers. The empty cans were washed and set back out for the driver to pick up to return to the farms.

When the time came to leave Louisiana to return to college, Mr. Patterson begged us school boys to continue working for him until the Causeway was finished. He promised us that we would make enough money to pay for our education by the time the Causeway was built. The Causeway was 24.6 miles in length, so we had no idea of how long it would take to complete it. Therefore, we four college boys returned to college.

Our First Car

AT THE END OF THE SUMMER, we purchased a 1948 Chrysler luxury sedan which was our first automobile. Dora and Nita returned to College Station with me where we rented a two bedroom house on the front end of Cooner Street owned by Dr. Jones. The house was an army barrack-style with a large water cooler in the living room window for cooling. It had a large fenced backyard where we kept our small dog Penny and a pair of leopard hounds given to me by a worker at Penn-Salt.

Both Began New Jobs in College Station

IN THE FALL OF 1955, Dora began her first job at the Park Cleaners across from the Texas A&M campus. In addition to attending classes, I started conducting glucose analyses of mesquite plants. I also became an animal caretaker for the pathology department's animal colony at the college. Dr. Pappy Burns raised dogs, rats, guinea pigs, and rabbits that were used in research and for teaching. I fed and watered the animals and cleaned the cages. Included in taking care of these animals, I was to be sure there were enough animals to supply the needs of the departments for their teaching. This meant that I was responsible for production. This was particular true of the guinea pigs, rats, and rabbits. When the pathology laboratories requirements were satisfied, all reproduction was stopped. Any surplus rabbits made their way to Cooner Street for table food.

Acquiring a job at the Bryan Penn-Salt Chemical Company required that I give up the other jobs. I worked for the chemical company which made cotton poison during my final two years of college beginning at 7:00 p.m. and working until 12 midnight seven days a week. I operated the tri-calcium arsenate production facility. This facility consisted of very large vats of nitric acid steam heated pots. I worked on a platform adjacent to the pots and had to watch the gauges and temperature as an ingredient was pumped into the pots. Various laboratory tests had to be conducted to determine when the end point of the chemical reaction had been reached. These procedures allowed me free time to study, getting in four hours of study during a five hour shift.

At the beginning of my junior year, the new veterinary college facility, west of the railroad tracks, was completed. We began classes there. Also, Dora began working as a Browsing Librarian at the Memorial Student Center while Nita attended Mrs. Adams' private day care operated in her home in Bryan. These facts made it necessary for us to acquire a second mode of transportation. I was fortunate enough to purchase a yellow Crosley convertible from a fellow veterinary student, Jimmy Bruce Smith. This provided me transportation to classes and to work.

The Chrysler "Wore Out"

IN DECEMBER OF 1957, Dora, Nita, and I started to Louisiana for the Christmas Holidays in our 1948 Chrysler. The Chrysler was a V-8 luxury sedan and very comfortable for traveling. We left late in the afternoon and were traveling at night on Texas Highway 105 between Cleveland and Beaumont, Texas. The car began to go slower, slower, and slower, regardless of attempts to get it to move faster. We pulled over on the side of the road where it quit running. After sitting there for quite some time while making several attempts to get it started again, it finally started. We proceeded on to Beaumont traveling at 20 miles an hour and arrived at the Beaumont Chrysler dealership around 6:00 a.m. We sat at the dealership and waited until 7:30 a.m. for them to open. They pulled the Chrysler into the shop. When the mechanics examined the motor, he found that in some manner the engine had swallowed two pistons on the right hand side and the other pistons were cracked. They could not believe that the car had cranked and run all the way into Beaumont. (Another miracle) "Thank you God!" We had purchased the car for $200.00 and sold it for junk for $160.00 after driving it for 30,000 miles.

I called Daddy at Mt. Hermon, Louisiana and reported what had happened and where we were. He drove to Beaumont and picked us up and took us to Louisiana.

While we were home for Christmas at Mt. Hermon, we borrowed $2,000.00 from Mr. T. H. Cutrer and purchased a 1957 Chevrolet car and a 1957 half-ton pick-up truck. These were the first new vehicles that we had ever owned. We returned to College Station from the Christmas holidays driving two new vehicles.

My Big Day Came!

ON MAY 24, 1958, I graduated A&M College of Texas with a Doctor of Veterinary Medicine Degree. My parents, Rev. and Mrs. Marvin Magee; Dora's parents, Mr. and Mrs. Earl Wilkes; and Dora's sister and brother-in-law, Mr. and Mrs. Quinlon McElveen from Louisiana attended my graduation with Dora and Nita. Dora remembers crying of joy during my entire graduation ceremony. Just prior to the graduation services, our furniture was loaded onto the Wilkes truck. The Crosley was loaded onto the bed of the pick-up truck. After my graduation, we all drove home to Louisiana in a caravan.

Entering Veterinary Practice in Tangipahoa Parish

IT IS WORTH NOTING that the $4,000.00 I eventually borrowed ($2,000.00 for vehicles and $2,000.00 for a down payment on the Amite property) was the total debt that I owed for 6 ½ years of college education and the means to start a private veterinary practice. We also owed the balance of $7,600.00 on the Amite property.

After settling down from our journey from Texas at my parents' house in Natalbany, La., we purchased a nine room house with several acres on Highway 16, two miles East of Amite, La. for $9,600.00. Amite is the county seat for Tangipahoa Parish. This house had an enclosed back porch which served as my clinic. We did surgery on a white enamel metal kitchen table. Grandma Bridges had come again to help us move. This was her first surgery to ever see, and she cried during the entire time.

We purchased a Jersey cow for milk for the house and housed her in a barn several yards away from the house. When I was away making early morning calls, Dora had to go down and milk the cow. Just about the time she got to the barn to milk, the telephone at the house rang. She had to leave the cow and run answer the telephone and then return to the barn to complete the milking. There was no such thing as a mobile phone at that time. The yellow telephone was mounted on the kitchen wall. After several months, she decided it would be more beneficial to put calves on the cow and purchase milk from the grocery store. She did not have to join an aerobics class during this time.

Nita loved animals, and we always had animals around. Nita's little tan dog Penny (of doubtful parentage) had four white feet. Upon graduating college and returning to Louisiana, Penny accompanied us nursing six puppies. In addition, we acquired four leopard hounds and one Catahoula and some kittens. I don't remember what happened to the puppies. We left the leopard hounds with my parents in Natalbany, La. The four leopard hound puppies died of a hepatitis virus. "Shorty," the Catahoula had resided with us in College Station, in Amite, La., and moved with us to Kentwood, La. In Kentwood, we lived on Highway 51. This highway was the main route to travel north or south before the interstate highway was completed. "Shorty" was apparently not very bright, as he was hit on several different occasions by automobiles traveling up and down highway 51. He survived these encounters but finally succumbed to a hit by an eighteen wheeler. After "Shorty" we had only Nita's in-house dogs.

The country farmers were very cordial, and appreciated my locating in the area. There was a large group of "freejacks" who farmed in the area south of Highway 16. These were people who were originally White and Black and had originated much earlier in history. They did not marry out of their clan. They were, as a group, very industrious and very successful cattle farmers. I enjoyed working for them. They always paid their bills immediately after I finished working on their animals. They were very friendly and would usually invite me into their houses for coffee after we had finished the task at hand. However, if they did not accept a person, that person never went back to their farm for any type of service.

One of these individuals worked as livestock supervisor for Mr. Gaston Laneau, on the Tangipahoa Tung Farm. Mr. Laneau was the son-in-law of the owner of the Zemurray Steam Ship line. The Zemurray's had steam ships that traveled world-wide shipping various produce to the United States. Leander was as good if not better with cattle and horses than any other person with whom I ever worked. He taught me a trick that I tried to pass on to the veterinary students at a later time. Sometimes his very large crossbred cows (Santa Getrudis x common beef cows) would calve and their teats would be too large for the calf to get

37

the teat into its mouth to nurse. This cow would be put into a squeeze chute and restrained. After cleaning the teats and cleaning his sharp pointed knife he would make a small puncture about one inch above the end of each teat into the teat canal. This procedure allowed the milk to drain from the teat when the calf started to nurse. Of course, draining the udder in this fashion allowed the calf to nurse. By the time the calf was six weeks of age, it would be large enough to enclose the teat in its mouth as it nursed, and by that time the puncture wound would have healed.

The Tangipahoa Tung farm was very successful, producing several tank cars of tung oil each year. The farm marketed about 300 yearlings each year. The farm also raised quarter horses and thoroughbred horses. Mr. Laneau raced both thoroughbred and quarter horses. He was a very successful farmer, but "slow horses and fast New Orleans women" resulted in his wife divorcing him, and he was removed from managing the farm

The Amite town people liked to party, and some were not really concerned with paying their veterinary bills. Many of the town people would borrow money from the local bank to take a vacation trip. I accumulated $1,800 in uncollected accounts in the first 18 months that I practiced in Amite. This led to a decision to move to a new location.

Relocated My Veterinary Practice in Kentwood, LA, Where I Practiced 32 Years

I LOOKED INTO RENTING an office in Franklinton, in Washington Parish. Dr. Robert Blades, Kentwood Louisiana, somehow knew that I was getting ready to leave the Amite area and called to see if I would come up and talk with him. Due to health reasons, Dr. Blades was getting ready to leave Kentwood and move to San Antonio, Texas, where he intended to practice in a companion practice with a class mate. He offered to sell me his house and a large two story building next to his house located on 4 lots. We talked about this offer and I told him that I had no money. I did have $2,000.00 equity in the Highway 16 property. He decided that, if I would liquidate the Amite property and give him the $2,000.00 that he would finance the house for me. I did not buy the two story building. With this deal made Dora, Nita and I moved to Kentwood to start over again in practice.

The office in Kentwood was in a very small room in the back of the house with a side door entrance into the office. All veterinary work was ambulatory in nature. Prior to accepting Dr. Blades offer, I visited with Dr. Jimmy Rimes who has a veterinary office about two blocks north of the Blades house. Dr. Rimes was very agreeable to my relocating to Kentwood. I did not want to move to Kentwood if that would cause a problem with Dr. Rimes. He noted that there was more veterinary work in this area than one veterinarian could take care of. We developed a relationship through the years that was very beneficial to both veterinarians. If he went out of town, I would take care of emergency calls from his clients, and if I went out of town he would return the favor for my clients. This relationship eventually led to consideration of our forming a partnership. We were progressing in a favorable vein when the question of the wives participating in the partnership was broached. Dr. Rimes's wife Nadine was a registered nurse who administered vaccination injections and on occasion attended to other companion animal procedures. My reply was that the wives would go to each veterinarian's respective house and not participate in the practice. Dr. Rimes was reluctant to do this, so the partnership never materialized, but we remained good friends.

It soon became apparent that the small office in the back room of the house was not working. There was a garage made of tin setting behind the house to the right. It sat on railroad ties and could be moved rather easily. I brought to the house to help us move the garage an ex-convict who was helping us at the D&D Dairy. We placed large poles under the frame of the garage and rolled the garage into place just behind our house. This gave us parking space where the garage had been and allowed the traffic to circle in front of the office and out the other end of the driveway. After Dora helped engineer the moving of the garage, the ex-convict told me that I should put her in charge of things. A small treatment /surgery room was added to the south of the main building. Companion animal cages were built in the back of the building and outside animal enclosed runs were added. The lot behind the new office was fenced and became a large animal area.

Mrs. Ertie Forrest was hired as a receptionist. She was the widow of Norman Forrest, and the mother of Dale, Earl, and Ivy Beryl Forrest. She was the grandmother of two who are close friends and family, Kathy Dale Forrest and Norman Craig Forrest, a nephew-in-law to us. Mrs. Ertie worked for me at least ten or twelve years before she retired. During her tour of duty with the veterinary practice, we started using two way Motorola radios, to stay in touch with the office. This prevented a lot of "telephone tag" and a lot of back tracking while out of the office on farm calls.

About 1962 I decided that life would be a lot easier if there were another veterinarian in the practice. Being in a rural veterinary practice meant that there were a lot of very early morning farm calls as well as late night farm calls. This fact meant that the family had to adjust to a difficult life style. I hired an Oklahoma State veterinary graduate to work in the practice with me. This individual was hired on a six month trial period, with the provision that at the end of the six months we would evaluate the practice and see if we were both satisfied with the arrangement. This young man had just married prior to coming to work with me. His wife was not happy with the practice and the town. She often complained that "Babe" (the name that she called him) had to get up too early in the morning. After five months of our arrangement, I paid him for the sixth months and allowed him to leave Kentwood. He later went to work with the Federal Government, and apparently had a successful career in the Federal Government service.

One of the experiences that led to his dismissal was the Cat Alford story. Babe went to Mr. Alford's dairy farm to assist in a calf delivery. Several months went by and Mr. Alford never paid his bill for the calf delivery assistance. I finally went to the Alford farm and inquired of Mr. Alford why he never paid the account. He answered "Don't you know what happened? The young man could not correct the problem with the delivery. He called Dr. Jimmy Rimes to come out and help with the delivery." Mr. Alford said that he did not feel like he owed me anything. I agreed with him.

Another story was the use of the two way radios to communicate. The veterinarians in Franklinton, Louisiana were also using two way radios and were on the same channel as our office. They often listened as Babe called in to Mrs. Ertie and had her to read to him over the air about some condition from the medical library. What great advertising!

Dr. Carl Keller Became My First Veterinary Partner

ABOUT TWO YEARS LATER, in 1964, Dr. Carl Keller joined the practice. Carl married Gail May soon after coming to Kentwood. They went on a honeymoon trip from Gonzales (near the Baton Rouge area) to Hammond Louisiana. They were gone for one week. The morning after coming back to Kentwood, I knocked on their front door to get Carl up. Gail has never let me forget waking them up at 5:00 a.m. their first morning in Kentwood. We formed a veterinary partnership that lasted for twenty five years, and about 1978 we also formed a real estate partnership that is still in force. Soon after the formation of the veterinary partnership it became apparent that the little office behind the Blades house in which Dora, Nita and I lived, was too small and the practice needed larger quarters. The Partnership rented the old Becker and Bass machine shop behind L.M. McDaniel's service station, which was at the corner of Highway 51 and Highway 38. We began to renovate this building into a companion animal clinic facing Highway 38 and a large animal facility behind the companion animal clinic opening on the south side of the building and facing onto a vacant lot. This building served as the "Kentwood Veterinary Clinic" until the practice was moved to a new clinic two miles north of Kentwood on Highway 51 where it is still in operation today.

During the time of my veterinary education, I never performed a rectal examination on a cow. This procedure was just not taught in the education at that time. Dr. Joe Dixon, reproduction professor, at the LSU Veterinary Medicine Department visited the Southeastern Area Dairy Farm every Tuesday to do reproductive palpation examinations. He was gracious enough to allow me to accompany him on these trips. Tuesday was my day off from the practice, so for the next six months I followed Dr. Dixon as he palpated the dairy cows. I learned how to do bovine female reproductive exams, and I learned the strategies to affect improvements in Dairy Herd Health.

My niece, Robin Fabre, during her high school days thought she would like to be a veterinarian. When she could get the time, she would come up to Kentwood from her home in Ponchatoula and ride with me on farm visits. On one occasion when she arrived home from Kentwood, Mary Jane (my sister) asked her "What does Uncle Derry do"? She replied, "The best way to describe what Uncle Derry does is that he is a cow 'gynecologist'."

LSU Senior Veterinary Students Preceptees in Our Practice

LSU GRADUATED THE FIRST veterinary medicine class of 1978. During the 1977-1978 school year our practice had five LSU veterinary senior students who each spent five weeks with our practice. This was done on a rotating basis, one student at a time staying with the practice. Our clinic had all the facilities necessary to house the students during their stay.

Kentwood Veterinary Clinic Herd Health Program

I WAS VISITING THE Houston Brown Dairy with two LSU dairy extension personnel one afternoon as they consulted with Mr. Brown about the management of his dairy. All they did was drink coffee and eat Mrs. Brown's cake. After they left, Houston was very upset that they never went to the dairy barn or even looked at the cows or the cow records. I asked Houston if he and his wife were going to start the afternoon milking, and if I could stay with them and evaluate some of the cows. This was the inception of the Kentwood Veterinary Clinic program named "Herd Health." We never advertised the program, but it eventually grew in size and scope to include a third partner into the practice. Kentwood Veterinary Clinic practitioners paid routine visits to 50 dairy herds in the area.

On these visits we evaluated by rectal palpation all the cows that had calved in the last 30 days: all the cows that had gone over 35 days from the last insemination with no return to estrus; any cow inseminated three or more times without becoming pregnant; and any cow that had no recorded estrus since calving. By our calculation and the calculations of others, we returned to the dairy farm $5.00 for every $1.00 spent on this program.

When I graduated Texas A&M School of Veterinary Medicine and located in Tangipahoa parish, there were six veterinarians within a 25 mile radius of Kentwood. As other veterinarians began to incorporate herd health programs into their practices, the number of veterinarians grew at a steady pace. In 1990 there were 25 veterinarians located in this same area. Most were mixed animal practices that included herd health practitioners. In 1958, there were 1453 dairies in the parish and the cattle population was listed as 63,000. Our practice area was located in Tangipahoa Parish and extended to St. Helena Parish to the west and Washington Parish to the east, plus three counties in Mississippi; Amite, Pike and Walthall. There were probably 150,000 cattle in the five surrounding counties and parishes. It is sad that today less than 200 dairies

are left in the whole state of Louisiana. The number of practicing veterinarians in this area has also decreased.

I cooperated with the LSU College of Veterinary Medicine, in their Large Animal Production medicine program. The school furnished our practice with a computer program for maintaining herd health records. Four of our dairy herds were included in this program. At the end of every herd health visit, the records were entered into the program and telephoned to the college's epidemiology department where various analytical evaluations were processed for their teaching and researching programs.

At one point in time, someone in the college's administrative area decided that they could not continue to cooperate with our practice unless at least one of us was a member of their faculty. I became an adjunct professor in the College's epidemiology department with an annual salary of One dollar. I gained valuable experience with computerized record keeping which served me very well when I was hired at Texas A&M.

Veterinary Practice Stories

"My Aggie Rings"

AT THE END OF MY sophomore year attending Texas Agricultural and Mechanical College of Veterinary Medicine, I received my "Aggie Ring." I had an immense sense of pride on that day. All college graduates seem to share a sense of pride upon receiving their rings when graduating from their chosen universities. This pride is especially true of the Aggies who receive their rings. They share a bond that goes beyond what many other university graduates do not understand. The Aggie Ring is a symbol of that bond.

Very soon after graduating from the Texas A&M College of Veterinary Medicine, I was doing a cesarean section on a cow. After I had finished suturing the incision, I realized that my Aggie ring was not on my finger. We looked everywhere for the ring but could not find it. I finally came to the conclusion that it was in the cow's abdominal cavity. I did not have the heart to reopen the incision and start groping through the abdominal cavity to see if I could find the ring.

My wife, knowing how much the ring meant to me, bought me a second "Aggie Ring." I did not learn from the first ring incident that the ring should have been removed while working cattle. A friend and client had several six-month old yearlings that needed to be vaccinated. He did not have any working facilities, such as a cattle chute or other ways to handle the yearlings. With the help of a neighbor, the yearlings were put into a small stable. These men caught and held the yearling while I vaccinated them. We identified the yearlings by tattooing the right ear and inserting a metal tag on the ear. When we had finished working the cattle, the stable was over shoe-top deep in cow manure. As I was washing up, I discovered that once again I had lost my ring. It was in that messy stable!

My client's sister heard about the lost ring. After I had gone on to make other farm calls, she retrieved a garden rake and proceeded to rake the whole stable until she found the ring. I was so happy to have the ring again. I decided that wearing a ring and working cattle were not compatible. The ring went into a special box and stayed there until I retired in 2007 and began wearing the ring again. This is why my ring which is now over 50 years in age still looks brand new.

"A Prophet Has No Honor in His Hometown"

One of my first farm calls in Kentwood was to the farm of a member of the Line Creek Baptist Church. This man and his wife had watched me grow up in the Line Creek community. After tending to the man's cow, I was invited up to the house for a cup of coffee which was in preparation for being paid for the farm call. As the farmer entered the house, he sang out to his wife. "Mother, Dr. Magee is here, and he and I would like a cup of coffee." As we entered the kitchen, the wife looked over at me and said in a loud voice; "Dr. Magee," and a slight pause, followed by "Why that's 'little ole Derry,'" and indeed to her I was still 'little ole Derry,' the young man who went to church with them and ate several Sunday dinners at their house. I appreciated the love and concern they always showed for me, Dora and Nita.

"Lucas Simmons, a Friend"

There were at least five of the Simmons boys who farmed in the Line Creek Community. Luke was the one who was instrumental in helping me raise dairy calves and later starting a dairy with these calves while I was still in high school at Mt. Hermon. Luke was familiar with the old time country remedies such as deworming cattle with Black Leaf 40 and Blue stone, using turpentine topically and internally, pushing a greasy rag down a cow's throat when the cow had lost her "cud," and last, but not the only remedy, boring a hole into the underside of the horn to relieve the "hollow horn."

A common agricultural practice was to allow the cattle to glean the corn fields after the major portion of the crop had been harvested. There were usually a number of very small corn ears, referred to as "nubbins." The cattle readily rooted them out and ate them.

Many times a cow that had recently calved would begin to become hypocalcemic. As the level of calcium in the blood began to fall, the cow would become uncoordinated. She would have uncontrolled muscle tremors and begin to grind her teeth in a chewing motion. Further decrease in the calcium blood levels would lead to torticollis (an "S" shaped curve of the neck) with the animal lying down and unable to rise. Eventually, the cow went into a coma followed by death. The old time remedy was to pump air into the udder. This was to inflate the udder and the pressure would drive calcium from the milk in the udder back into the blood stream. The modern treatment was to give calcium solutions intravenously by slow drip. The symptoms explained above would be reversed and the animal would usually become ambulatory in a short period of time.

One day Luke called and said that he had a cow that was "down" in his corn field. I drove to his farm and began to administer the I.V. calcium solution. This cow had become hypocalcemic while eating corn nubbins, and as she went down, she still had a corn nubbin in her mouth. As the I.V. calcium solution began to reverse the hypocalcemia, she involuntarily began to work her mouth as if chewing. Luke's excited comment was "Lord it's a miracle, she is already eating."

On one occasion Luke and a group of his buddies were talking and telling stories. Luke said that all his wife, Mary Ellen, ever did was ask for money. One of his buddies asked, "Luke, what does she need the money for and what does she do with the money?" His reply, "I don't know. I have never given her any."

"The $500.00 Cup of Coffee"

We answered calls for veterinary assistance 24 hours a day, 7 days each week. We took turns being on call. When the telephone rang at midnight or very early in the morning and a high pitched nasal voice said, "Miss Mageeeeeeeeee." Ray had a cow that needed assistance in some manner. Dora would say "Hello Ray," and he would reply, "How did you know it was me calling?" Ray and a brother were bachelors who lived with a sister. They all lived and worked together on their dairy farm. They were very fond of their cattle and did not want anything to hurt the cows. They believed that every effort should be extended to save a life. The cows calved in a relatively large wooded area. It was very often necessary to search in the woods pasture to find the cow that needed assistance. Ray's brother was "shell shocked" in World War II. One night, as I was attempting to assist the cow by flash light, a sudden imaginary battle of epic proportions took place in the dark. The "shell shocked" brother was battling the "Japs" all over the woods.

On various occasions, Ray would invite me to come to his house (a very nice brick home) to drink coffee. In his kitchen, the cats had to be swept off the counter and onto the floor. Water for making coffee would be put on to boil, so I knew it would be alright to drink the coffee. There were cats everywhere in the kitchen, and one must not hurt any of them. Ray kept a book of blank bank checks and would say, "Doc, make you out a check for $500.00." No balance was every kept in the check book, but every check that we ever received was honored by the bank. On the way from the cow pasture to the house, I would radio the office and tell them that I was on my way to drink the $500.00 cup of coffee.

"The Farmers Home Administration (FHA)"

The FHA is a federal government program that is supposed to insure an adequate food supply for the nation. It is my opinion that most government programs fail in a miserable way or succeed beyond expectations to the detriment of the industry they are supposed to help. The FHA supports individuals who are unable to finance a farming operation through conventional methods. The program lends money but does nothing to educate the people who borrow from the organization.

The history of these farming operations is such that the FHA borrowers would usually be bankrupt by the end of seven years. One story illustrates this opinion. A young man whose brother was a very successful dairy farmer started a dairy farm with the help of the FHA in Pike County, Mississippi. By the end of his seven years, he was bankrupt. We never received any money on accounts owed to the Clinic by him or others in the bankrupt proceedings. This young man was a very nice individual but incompetent in managing a dairy farm. He moved into Tangipahoa Parish on his father-in-law's farm and with the help of the Tangipahoa Parish FHA started another dairy farm. His ledger in our veterinary office was flagged with, "Extend no credit." However, one day I noticed that he had bought some supplies and had not paid cash for them. I finally got his account back to zero and went to see him to inform him that any future veterinary services would be on a cash basis. We had been dealing with this young man for over ten years at this point. I told him that I had come to apologize to him. His response, "Oh, Dr. Magee, you have been very good to me." I replied, "I know that, but I have extended to you in the past more credit than you could pay, and I have come to promise you that I will not put you in that position again. You are now on notice that all services and supplies will be cash only." Would you believe that by the end of his seven years on his father-in-law's farm he was bankrupt again? Our veterinary practice saw this happen on several occasions.

"G.T. Patterson's White Tennessee Walker Stallion"

Mr. G.T. Patterson, whom I had worked for on the Causeway across Lake Ponchartrain while a student, had a prized White Tennessee Walking Stallion that cut his Achilles tendon. When the horse tried to move, the foot turned up and his fetlock (ankle) touched the ground. A veterinary practitioner anesthetized the horse and did a beautiful job of suturing the tendon, wound and applying a fiberglass cast. But when the horse began to recover from the anesthesia, it began to thrash about and upon rising broke the cast and ripped all the sutures out.

Mr. Patterson called and asked if I would come and take a look at the horse. I did and told him I could fix the horse. He asked what the amount of fee would be. I answered that I would correct the problem for $250.00. He responded that he had no use for a crippled horse, but would go double or nothing if I were willing to take that arrangement. I replied that it was a deal, and we shook hands to confirm the deal. There was no paperwork, no notary fee, no lawyer fee involved, just an honest hand shake to complete the deal.

In practice I had the good fortune of living a short distance from a retired master farrier who had spent a life time on the Indiana trotting race tracks. He had a large repertoire of treatments for all manner of foot and leg injuries. After bringing the horse to Kentwood by trailer, I went to Happy Ingles, the retired master farrier, and told him what I needed. He built a steel brace to hold the horse's foot that went up above the cut Achilles tendon with several braces that went one half of the way around his leg. Leather belts were fastened into the braces to hold the leg in a firm position. The wound was then wrapped to hold the tendon in place.

After about two months, the tendon and wound had healed enough for us to try the leg without the brace. The horse limped, but the leg and foot stayed in proper position. After another month, we began to exercise him by leading him around the back lot and finally, I got in the back of Dr. Keller's pickup truck. As he drove, we began to lead the horse on the road to be sure that his leg had healed. Many of the residents in our small town were surprised to see a pickup truck traveling down the road with a white horse pacing behind the truck. Upon returning the horse to Mr. Patterson, I collected the $500.00. If one accounts for all the time spent with this horse, I don't think that we really made any money, but there was the satisfaction of completing a problem that others had failed to correct.

Companion Animal Practice

"Cats"

Our clientele was primarily farm animals, horses and cows, but companion animals, cats and dogs, were part of the practice. A former librarian at Mississippi College who late in life married the owner of the Kentwood Chevrolet dealership. She had a tri colored mother cat and a yellow tiger striped kitten that she brought to the Kentwood Veterinary Clinic for their periodic care. As time went on, her husband died and she began to experience dementia. But, she still kept her cats. One day when I came into the office after a farm call, I was told that her daughter brought in the cats and paid to have them euthanized. Now this was a problem. I thought that it was possible that the owner might have a good day and miss her cats. I solved the problem. I took the cats home with me, and they became our house cats. I thought that if the owner ever came for her cats that I could tell her that they were at my house for their safe keeping until she returned to pick them up. She never came for her cats, and they died of old age at our house.

One of our local dentists loved cats. He would pick up any stray cat that came around his house and bring it to the clinic for veterinary care. At the time we had a young veterinarian practicing with Dr. Keller and me whose priority was cattle, but he loved cats almost as much as cattle. He and the dentist became close friends during the time the young veterinarian practiced at the clinic. One Sunday when I was the "on call" veterinarian, the dentist called and said that one of his cats was sick. When he brought the cat to the clinic, I examined the cat and determined that one side of the lungs was filled with fluid. I told the dentist my diagnosis and put the cat in the kennel. I started it on antibiotics and told the dentist that I knew that he and the young veterinarian were good friends and when the office opened Monday Morning I would have the young veterinarian evaluate the cat. This was acceptable to him. I started a patient record and recorded my diagnosis. Monday morning arrived and the young practitioner made radiographs and took blood samples from the cat. When he finished his workup, he came over to our private office and began to question me. "How did you make that diagnosis?" he asked. Not to be smart, I told him that I listened to the lungs with my stethoscope. This illustrates the difference between older practitioners who had to depend on their five senses and the younger generation who had become accustomed to using a lot of ancillary tests to make a diagnosis. Perhaps my twenty-one years of practice (at that time) could explain the differences between us. He later made the statement to some students, "Dr. Magee taught me how to practice." I might also add that he brought our practice up to modern standards. It was a win-win relationship.

"Dogs"

Every farm client had at least one stock dog. Most hunters had one or more dogs. These dogs were not pedigreed animals but were usually valued members of the family. There were also the family pets. There were three bachelor brothers who had a dairy west of the town of Kentwood. Their sister had a dachshund that developed epilepsy. We put the dog on primidone, a medicine that controls the convulsive seizures typical of this disease. The owner administered the medicine daily for seven or eight years until the pet died at the old age of 12 years. Later at Texas A&M, I was told that I had put the dog on the wrong medicine. He might have lived to be 25 years of age on the proper medication, but I doubt that was the case.

Dr. Keller was the primary surgeon at the Kentwood Veterinary Clinic. He did many elective surgeries and also repaired simple clean bone breaks. This was sterile surgery using sterile instruments and sterile attire. The compound fractures were referred to clinics that had the advanced equipments necessary to repair the fractures. This special equipment required a very large cash outlay of various supplies that were kept in a clinic's inventory.

Leaving Louisiana Practice

IN THE OLD TESTAMENT, refer to Deuteronomy 32:11 and Job 39: 27-28. These references refer to the eagles in Israel. The Bible, in Job verifies that the eagles build their nest on rocky ledges high on the side of cliffs. The Deuteronomy reference calls attention to the fact that GOD will use natural means to cause his followers to move in the direction HE desires, especially when they have become very comfortable in their present situations and do not wish to move. The eagles start to build their nest by pushing large sticks into cracks of the ledge. Then they add smaller branches around these large sticks. Finally, they pad the nest with grass, leaves and feathers to have a safe, comfortable nest. The eggs hatch, and the young eaglets grow very fast. As they develop feathers, they begin to hop around in the nest. When they have developed their full flight feathers they will sit on the edge of the nest and flap their wings. They have no intention of leaving the nest. Why should they when the parents bring them food and they are very comfortable living in the nest? But unless they leave the comfort of the nest, they will not experience the joy of flight.

Finally, the mother gets tired of this situation and begins to dismantle the nest. As she proceeds to destroy the nest, the young eagles have only the large sticks on which to sit. This is very uncomfortable for them, and they finally have to spread their wings and leave the nest area. They then enjoy the freedom of flight that they were destined to enjoy.

(Reference site:
<http://www.eagleflight.org/cybersermon/growing_church/eagl>)

Searching For New Opportunities

DEUTERONOMY 32:11 SAYS:

*"Like an eagle that stirs up its nest and hovers over its young,
that spreads its wings to catch them"*

In this story, Moses compares the eagles to GOD's leadership of the Israelites and how he makes them uncomfortable if they will not move when HE commands them to move. Just like the young eagles, we have to be *made* to leave the life area with which we have become comfortable when GOD says it is time to move on.

Toward the end of the 1980s, it was becoming evident that the area would no longer support four veterinarians-three in KVC and the other veterinarian, Dr. A.J. Rimes. The numbers of dairies were declining. There did not seem to be a lot of interest by the KVC veterinarians in developing the companion animal practice to help make up for the decreased farm animal revenue. I had now been in practice for over thirty years. If the farm animal-practice which included dairy, beef, and horses were to be expanded, the area of service would have had to be increased one hundred miles in all directions. This option was not attractive to me because it meant that farm trips would make it necessary to stay away from home for extended periods of time. I began to explore opportunities outside the KVC practice.

The first opportunity that I investigated was with the Federal Government. The Federal Government had advertised for thirty-five veterinarians to be trained in foreign animal disease pathology at Plum Island. This facility is a self contained institution where foreign animal diseases are investigated. The

Pathologist would also be responsible for animal inspection at various USA border inspection sites and in some foreign animal nations. I made the cut down to seventy applicants. I attended an appointment in New Orleans with a Human Resource female from a northern state and a recent female veterinarian graduate of the Black Tuskegee University. I guess I did not do well on this interview. The Tuskegee graduate told me at the end of the interview that if she had cattle to work I would certainly be in line for the job. This statement inferred that I did not meet the criteria for the position. Reflecting on this, I was probably too old for them to consider me. However, as later events would show, this was a blessing! I left New Orleans and went home to resume veterinary practice.

Kentwood Veterinary Clinic Provided Practice Experience to LSU Senior Veterinary Students

DURING THE LATE 1970s, Louisiana State University finally began the four year veterinary education, graduating their first veterinarians in 1978. During the students' senior year in school, they would go to various private practices for five weeks of interning with the private practitioners in that practice. KVC had five of these interns (or externs as they were called) during the 1977-78 year. One of these was Dr. Allen Roussel. Allen was very bright and a few months after his graduation, he joined our practice. Allen practiced with Dr. Keller and me for three years, after which he decided to continue his education, acquiring a master's degree from Purdue Veterinary School. He went to West Virginia as a large animal instructor. Following his time at West Virginia, he moved on to become an instructor in the Texas A&M College of Veterinary Medicine.

Dr. Bernard Trappey was also one of these interns. After graduation from veterinary school he went back to practice in his hometown in South Louisiana. After Dr. Roussel left our practice, we invited Dr. Trappey to join the practice, which he did. Dr. Trappey is still practicing at Kentwood Veterinary Clinic, where he is now the owner of the practice. In May 2009 Dr. Justin Roberts graduated the LSU School of Veterinary Medicine and now practices in the Kentwood Veterinary Clinic with Dr. Trappey.

Dr. Tom Green, Livonia, Louisiana, was an intern in our practice during his senior year at LSU. One cold day there was a calf delivery on the side of a hill. Tom struggled for a long time trying to correct the presentation of the calf. He finally turned to me and said "Dr. Magee, I have struggled as long as I can. You will have to take over this delivery." I told him; "Tom, when you done all that you can do, don't stop. Keep going." He continued and finally delivered the calf. After graduating veterinary school, he began a very successful practice in his home town of Livonia. He also became a politician a few years later and was elected to the Louisiana State Senate from his home district. After he was elected to the state senate, we met at a Louisiana State Veterinary Association meeting. He remarked to me that he had never forgotten the admonishment he received on the side of that cold hill trying to deliver that calf. The advice had become a motto to him to always keep in the back of his mind, regardless the task.

Dr. Christine Navarre was an intern in our practice. Christine's farther, Dr. Jim Beatty, is a very good friend of our family. I was honored to have her spend time in our practice. Of all our interns Christine was one of the most competent of them. She is the only intern that I allowed to palpate cattle without my checking their results. After graduation she did an internal medicine residency at TAMU with Dr. Roussel. After the residency, she took a Clinical position teaching in the Large Animal Clinic at the Auburn School of Veterinary Medicine. While I was teaching in Texas, we attempted to hire Christine as a tenure track professor in our Large Animal Clinic. We were sad that she declined the position. She is now the Louisiana State Extension Veterinarian. Her duties cover the whole state.

It was while working with these students that I found that I truly loved working with the students. During the latter time of 1989, Allen was in charge of a search committee to fill a vacancy for a Clinical Assistant Professor in the Texas A&M Large Animal Clinic. The duties would consist of taking senior veterinary students to the Eastham prison unit to work on their 1200 cow dairy. I do not know how Allen knew that I might be interested in making a move, but he contacted me about the position. During his first contact with me, Texas A&M was already negotiating with two candidates. I did not wish to get into a "horse race" for the position, so I said to him, "TAMU should finish their business with these two candidates, and if TAMU were not successful with either of the two candidates then give me a call, and we would talk more about the position." Both candidates were eliminated. Allen called and suggested that I prepare a short presentation and bring Dora to College Station to have a vacation at TAMU's expense.

We included my mother on this trip and proceeded to College Station for my second visit to the college since May, 1958, my graduation date. My presentation to the College was an analogy relating the work of a dairy practitioner to that of a football team and its coach. My short seminar was well received, and then the round of visits to various administration individuals began. These interviews were positive with one exception. The dean was out of town and two assistants met with me. One of the men was very cordial, but the other one was confrontational. I left that interview thinking that all was not well and that the position really needed further consideration by the College. I relayed this thought to my conductor and to the department head. I had been a private veterinary practitioner for 32 years and had really been working for myself ten years before graduating veterinary school. An assistant academic dean did not impress me. I then went back to the motel and told Dora and mother that we needed to get back to Kentwood. I thought there would be no further contact about the position.

Much to my surprise, about ten days later a letter arrived at my home address. The letter was from the assistant dean who was not impressed with me in our interview. He said that prior to my interview he had not read my resume and had not read the advertisement for the position. After reviewing these documents, he apologized for the interview. He stated that I should accept the offer of the position, and if I would accept the offer, I should come by his office for another visit and a cup of coffee with him and his staff. I visited with Dora and told her that since this was the kind of individuals with whom I would be working that we should accept the invitation to become part of the Texas A&M University, College of Veterinary Medicine, Large Animal Medicine and Surgery Department.

I called the Department Head and told him that I would accept the appointment, but the salary was very low. He said that that they had already added $3,500.00/year to the previously quoted salary. Later, as I visited with the Department Head, I told him that the salary was still low, but I would work with it for one year. I also stated that I was sure if my work were satisfactory, he would take care of me at the beginning of the next year. I got a 23% raise at the start of my second year and continued to get modest raises for the next 17 years in the department.

When I arrived in College Station, I was driving our large red Beauville Chevrolet van. This was during the last few days of February, 1990. I was to start work April 1, 1990. I had loaded a few clothes and other essentials in the van and drove alone to College Station. Dora remained in Kentwood to finish her contract with the Tangipahoa Parish School Board, teaching in the Special Education Department at Kentwood High School. We had rented a unit in the Longmire Drive Condo group, College Station, Texas. The name condo does not really describe the unit which was a very modest three room condo with a small bathroom unit. As I drove up, the next door neighbor and his wife and small child were sitting in front of the building. As I opened the back of the van and began to unload my meager belongings, the young couple scooped up their child and disappeared into their unit. They were really frightened of their new next door neighbor. I guess the fact that I only had an air mattress to sleep on did not alleviate their apprehension. Later after Dora came to College Station, the couple became very close friends with our family.

ACADEMIA

VETERINARY PRACTICE AT TEXAS A&M SCHOOL OF VETERINARY MEDICINE

"SODIUM IODIDE, FORMALDEHYDE, AND ANTIHISTAMINE"

EARLY IN MY PRIVATE PRACTICE years, I had the occasion to visit with a veterinarian who had served in the Calvary during World War I. In our conversation, he told me about the use of Sodium Iodide and also Formaldehyde in treating the Calvary horses. In his era in the Calvary, no antibiotics were available to treat infections, and there was only a limited supply of Sulfonilamide. They used the Sodium Iodide (which is a source of iodine) intravenously to treat infections. During the time of my student and early private practice years, Sodium Iodide was listed as a treatment for "Lumpy Jaw " in cattle and in horses for various nonspecific infections. As I worked with the herd health programs, one problem was with repeat breeders. Some cows would have regular estrus cycles but would never get pregnant. One rectal palpation finding revealed that after estrus the uterus never returned to a normal inter-estrus state. The uterus always seemed to have fluid dispersed throughout the total reproductive tract. I do not remember why, but I tried treating these cows with I.V. Sodium Iodide. I recommended skipping insemination during the next estrus cycle, and then breeding the cow on the following estrus cycle. To my delight and surprise, about 80% of these cows became pregnant on that insemination. I never published any report on this treatment because I had never conducted an "ACADEMICALLY" accepted double blind research project. However, I did share the treatment with several of my board certified Theriogenologist colleagues in the Large Animal Department at TAMU. One of them asked, "How does this treatment work?" I replied that I really did not know how it worked, but I supposed that it kicked the white blood cells in the rear end and excited them to make their greatest effort. At some time later, a research project was conducted, and it was proved that the Sodium Iodide I.V. did actually stimulate the white blood cells to perform at their maximum ability. Out in the boondocks, you just used programs that worked and did not spend a lot of time speculating about why they were successful.

In our practice in Kentwood, Louisiana, all three veterinarians adopted the practice of injecting an antihistamine I.V. which also contained one gram of thiamin during the final part of a calcium drip in downer cows. Again, I do not remember the origin of this therapy, but it was usually successful in getting these downer cows to regain the standing and walking ability. A few minutes after injecting the antihistamine, the cow would begin to move her tail back and forth, move her legs, stand up, urinate, deficate, and walk off. The Texas A&M dairy had a jersey cow that had been recumbent for three days. She was alert to her surroundings but would not make any attempt to stand up. I accompanied one of the theriogenologists to the dairy the next day. I asked if I could treat the cow and was granted permission to treat the cow. I dripped the calcium, thiamine I.V. and topped it off with twenty cc's of Triplenamine. In a few minutes, as described above, the cow stood and walked off. As we were going back to the Clinic, the Therio person asked, "How does that work?" My response (not to be "smart") was that I did not know how it worked, but it just causes them to stand up. I did not know the mechanism of the therapy but had used the treatment in private practice for 25 to 30 years.

Many times after calving, a cow would have udder edema which sometimes caused small capillaries to rupture leading to bloody milk. If this bleeding were severe, the milk might stay bloody for up to a week or more. Ten cc's of Formaldehyde added to a calcium drip given I.V. would cause the vessels to clot and the milk to clear up in one to two days. This same therapy was used in the Calvary horses if they had small hemorrhages that would not clot. As mentioned above, this therapy was relayed to me by the old Calvary veterinarian who had practiced in World War I. However, the Formaldehyde therapy was not used in the Texas A&M Large Animal Clinic until after I arrived to practice there.

I had occasion to work with the TAMU Dairy while at the University. The on-site dairy manager did not like to cooperate with the TAMU veterinary school but would do so when absolutely necessary. One of the Dairy Professors was agreeable to participating with the TAMU veterinarians. I visited with him, and we set up a program to improve the udder health at the dairy. At that time, the dairy was milking 200 cows. Milking procedures were introduced and some time was spent getting the student help to adjust to the new milking routine. The milking parlor held 12 cows at a time in a herringbone configuration. The new routine was to use a teat dip on three cows at the time. A separate paper towel was used on each of the three cows to wipe the dip off and stimulate the milk let down. The mechanical milking machine was then attached, being sure that the milking machine was attached to the under within 90 seconds of starting the teat preparation. Then the next three cows were prepared in the same manner. Two students were in the barn; one at the back of the barn and one at the front. This procedure contributed to improved production by making use of the oxytocin stimulation.

Every cow that calved was cultured the day of calving. This identified any presence of mastitis bacteria in the udder. If a mastitis causing pathogen was identified, the cow was immediately treated for three consecutive days, both intravenously and inter-mammary. This allowed the cow to return to the milking string within seven days. The end result: after one year on this program, the dairy's production average went up from 17,000 pounds of milk per cow per year to 21,000 pounds of milk per cow per year. The protein and fat content of the bulktank milk improved to a level that the dairy received a premium for its daily production. The dairy income increased $35,000.00 with very little added expense to the operating cost.

I experimented with the use of ozone to treat some cases of mastitis. Now ozone is highly oxidative, causing destruction of protein when it comes in contact with the protein. I dissolved ozone in cold saline solution which limited the amount of ozone concentration in the solution. This level made it safe to expose the solution to living tissue. I would generate a pint of the ozonated saline solution and infuse it into an infected udder. This solution killed any and all bacteria it contacted plus it denatured any toxins it contacted. With this treatment, I was able to successfully treat environmental bacterial infections and certain Streptococcus infections. The ozone did not penetrate into the udder tissues, so it was not effective in removing bacteria that had already penetrated into the udder tissues. The significance of this therapy was that animals treated with the ozonated saline returned to normal milk production within seven days of the therapy. There was no milk withdrawal time because no antibiotics were used in the therapy. The drawback to the therapy is that the solution had to be generated fresh each time a cow was treated. The ozone returned to oxygen within 30 minutes of being generated.

I wanted to initiate a research project using this therapy, but was unable to do so because of governmental regulation. The oversight committee for the use of animals in research wanted to know how I intended to dispose of the animal after their use in a research program. I stated that I intended to return the animal to profitable production after therapy. This was unheard of by the committee. They just could not comprehend the nature of cows in a dairy. All animals in a research project had to be disposed of when the project was completed. The oversight committee finally said they would approve the project, but the entire dairy would have to become an approved Laboratory Facility. The operation of the dairy would not be possible as a Laboratory Facility.

Veterinary Senior Students Rotation at the Texas Department of Criminal Justice (TDCJ)

WORKING FOR THE Large Animal Medicine and Surgery Department, College of Veterinary Medicine, Texas A&M University was very nice. They furnished me an office, a very slow computer and a floppy disk program, clothes to wear at the office, khaki pants, and a few coverall suits. On my first day at the clinic, I met Dr. Young, who was in charge of the Texas Department of Corrections Senior rotation. This senior clinical rotation was the result of an interagency Memorandum of Agreement between the Agriculture Division of the Texas Department of Criminal Justice (TDCJ) and The Texas A&M University College of Veterinary Medicine's Large Animal Department. He drove over from the Ferguson Unit in a Chevrolet station wagon that was to become my transportation. He handed me the vehicle keys, and I drove him back to the TDCJ Ferguson Unit. His only admonition that I remember is to be careful of starting any programs with the prison system because you will not recognize the program when the prison agricultural employees start to use the program. This word of advice became very true. It is worthy to note that Dr. Young was a "ward boss in the democratic political party" and a bishop in the Mormon Church. His wife had died of cancer, and he was very cranky most of the time. The perception was that he did not like female students and really did not like any student. For these characteristics, he and I did not have a very good relationship. I am Southern Baptist and conservative with an independent political outlook on all political matters.

His primary area of responsibility was the swine production program. He had improved the swine production over the previous 14 years that he was associated with the TDCJ system, raising the number of pigs weaned per sow from nine pigs weaned per sow to 14 pigs weaned per sow. My primary responsibility was the 1200 cow dairy on the Eastham Unit and the various beef cow units on 16 prison units. Dr. Young was to continue the care of the horses and the dogs. I made the announcement that I was working with the system to take care of the dairy but that I would help out with the beef cattle when I could. You might guess what happened. My first day with the students was to pregnancy test the beef cattle on one of the units. The ag workers on that unit never let me forget that announcement that I made the first day that I came to work with the prison system.

I took students to the Eastham Unit four days a week, Monday–Thursday. At the dairy, we palpated the cows that needed to be evaluated, diagnosed medical problems, treated the problems that were diagnosed, and established milk withdrawal times for any cows that received medication. Prior to the time that this dairy was established, small dairies were maintained on many of the prison farm units. The Agriculture Administration decided that all of these small dairies should be closed and the cows moved to the Eastham unit. The move was not well thought out, and the health and welfare of the cows were not adequately designed. There were 16 strings on concrete with clay loafing arrears. The only time the cows were allowed off the concrete was when they were dried off the last two months of their pregnancy. The prison system had all the dirt moving equipment that would have been needed and an open field north of the dairy that could have been renovated, but the administration never chose to do this. There were many leg injuries and foot problems. But, in spite of all efforts, this dirt loafing area was never constructed. As a result, many cows were lost.

Downer Cows at Coefield

THE DAIRY OPERATED until November, 1993. During the time we were working in the dairy, 50 new or first calf heifers, were added every month to the milking herd. This meant that over 43 months 2,150 new animals were added to the herd. Yet, because of gross mismanagement and when the herd was dispersed, there were only 800 cows left. This is a perfect example of the "Peter Principle" at work. This principle says that employees (who may be very competent when placed at work) are promoted to jobs of greater responsibility, until they rise to the level of their incompetence. This was very true at the local level of the dairy administration. One illustration of this point is: an employee working with the recently calved cows kept one cow in the sick pen for 25 days because he forgot every day and administered antibiotics to the cow when he was not supposed to use antibiotics on the cow.

There were 14 "free world" employees working in various positions in the dairy. Their local supervisor was a nice young man who had never worked an employee before being hired at the dairy. He had no idea how to plan and supervise the work of these 14 employees. A previous dairy supervisor was so problematic that one half of the work force quit during one week's time. It was at the end of his duty as dairy supervisor that no person was available to supervise the dairy. The prison administration decided to turn the operation over to me. I acted as dairy supervisor for five months. I think that it is worthy of note that during my five months as management supervisor:

1. There were no downer cows;
2. There were no recently fresh cows with retained placentae;

3. There were no recently fresh cows with ketosis.
4. By completely changing the way the cows were fed during the dry period and in the first few weeks after calving, the number of cows giving over 100 pounds of milk daily increased from an occasional one cow to over twenty per month.
5. There were no "left displaced abomasums."

Contrast this to the last week the dairy operated. The students and I did eleven "left displaced abomasal" surgeries. The drastic increase in the number of surgeries was due to the manner the last young dairy supervisor fed the dry cows and the recently fresh cows. The prison administration was very worried that the way I fed the cows was going to result in a disaster. They thought that getting the cows to increase production in such a dramatic fashion was going to burn the cows up. They did not realize that they were stopping the cows' production by limiting the nutrients in their feed and adding to the cows' metabolic health problems. The young dairy supervisor did not understand how to feed the cows. He just would not ask for nor take any counsel from me or anyone else. Under this young man's supervision, the dairy was projected to lose five million dollars in the next year and because of this loss projection, the dairy was terminated. The facility housing the dairy was turned into a swine feeder slab operation.

In 1993, based on my background with the dairy industry, I was appointed a member of the Texas A&M Team that joined the Land of Lakes Team and the United States Department of Agriculture (USDA) in conducting a survey of the dairy industry in Mexico. We covered the entire country of Mexico visiting the dairy industry that existed there.

After the dairy was terminated, I was fortunate that the beef cattle enterprise workers thought enough of my work that they asked the prison administration to keep me employed to work with the beef cattle. When I started to work on the contract between TDCJ and the Large Animal Medicine and Surgery Department, April 1, 1990, TDCJ had 6,000 cows and 550 bulls. Through the cooperation of the Agricultural Division Administration, the many farm workers working on 16 different prison farm units and various TAMU agricultural support persons, we were able to increase the number of breeding females to 15,000 animals and actually reduce the number of bulls to slightly over 300 animals. By using two breeding seasons for the heifer development farm and three breeding seasons for the cows, we were able to achieve an 88% pregnancy rate for the system.

I changed the bull breeding soundness exam from the use of the "Wiggle" test to a recognized breeding soundness procedure.

First, the "Wiggle" test involved collecting a semen sample on a microscope slide looking at the slide with the naked eye. If any movement were seen, then the bull was declared sound. The Society of Theriogenology had recognized procedures for evaluating bull fertility: microscopic evaluation of the semen sample for motility, and also dyeing a small part of the sample and evaluating the dried sample for specific morphology defects. A compromise with the prison was reached concerning bulls that did not pass the breeding soundness exam. If a bull failed the exam on two evaluations over two breeding seasons, he was considered a cull and was disposed through auction. In addition to the breeding soundness exam, the bulls were also cultured for *Trichomonas foetus*. This is a disease that is transmitted during breeding to the females by infected bulls, causing the infected cow to abort the fetus. The disease resides on the surface of the prepuce, in crypts of the epithelium. The bull has no ill effects from the presence of the protezoa. Any bull that was positive for "Trick" was immediately culled. About 35 % of the bull population was culled because of the Trick infection. As the bull health was improved, the pregnancy percentage increased from about 60% to 88%.

In the early days of the beef cattle enterprise with the prison if a cow did not calve, one ear was cut off. If at some later year, this cow again missed having a calf her other ear was cut off and then the cow was culled. There was no mistake in looking for cows to sell if they did not have any ears. There is a problem with this philosophy. The average yearly cost to maintain an adult cow in Texas is $285.00. It is predicted that if a cow misses one year of calving, she must then produce four straight years to make a profit from her calves. It is very unlikely for this to happen. If during this four year period, she again missed having a calf there is no way she will ever return to be a profitable unit, and the farm has lost the cost of maintaining her in hopes that she will become a profitable unit. The prison kept books on how many animals a farm had on its premises. They did not do a bottom line profit and loss statement. With this type of fuzzy accounting, it was a very hard job to get the farm managers to sell a cow. I worked with the managers for seventeen years, and as the old managers retired and were replaced with younger managers, the profit and loss style of management was gradually introduced.

The livestock production programs were part of the TDCJ Agriculture program. The prison system grew every product that could be grown in Texas. The system planted cotton, which was harvested and processed into white cloth. All the prisoners' clothes' were made with the white cloth at various prison units. Every manner of field crop, row crop, garden crop or other food crops were grown and utilized to feed the prisoners. In addition there were cattle enterprises, horse enterprises, swine enterprises, egg production enterprises and dog enterprises. The average annual cost of the agriculture program was thirty-five million dollars, but the annual return was recorded at forty-five million dollars, a very nice profit for prison agriculture. This endeavor is the best kept secret in Texas. The public news press is always looking for scandals. The papers never report on this type of good news.

A Veterinarian's *Wife*

Growing Up in the Mt. Pisgah Community

GROWING UP IN THE MT. PISGAH community allowed me to grow up around grandparents, uncles, aunts, cousins, and good neighbors who were very compassionate toward one another. They helped mold my character and helped instill in me a strong work ethic. It also gave me the chance to learn many things about what our parents and grandparents did to provide for their families and to make their farms productive. I saw first-hand how hard my parents worked each day starting before sunrise and ending after dark to provide for our family. As I observe my parents' children, grandchildren, and great-grandchildren, I see their love and compassion for their families. I also see a strong work ethic in them as they work in their jobs, their homes, yards, and communities.

The Mt. Pisgah community in Washington Parish is located in the heart of the piney woods in southeast Louisiana and in the northeast corner of the Florida Parishes. This community, along with other communities in these parishes, was made up of English-speaking settlers from the hill country of the western Carolinas, Virginia, and Georgia. My great-grandfathers and other settlers chose rather fertile land to settle on because the piney woods reminded them of their homes in the East. These settlers produced almost all of their necessities except for salt. My grandparents and parents even grew coffee. As herdsmen, the settlers let their hogs and cattle run loose and graze in the piney woods surrounding their cleared and cultivated lands.

The early settlers usually built their homes of logs and near creeks. They cleared land for vegetable gardens and fields for growing corn, rice, cane, and cotton. They canned fruits and vegetables for food during the winter. Cotton was used to make clothing and for income. They planted fruit trees that produced apples, pears, peaches and persimmons. They grew chickens for meat and eggs, cows for milk and meat, and hogs for meat and lard. Each farmer had a smoke house used to smoke the pork to preserve it for future meals.

Burch Grandparents Provided Support

My life began as I was born the second child and daughter of Earl Samuel Wilkes, Sr. and Willie Marie Burch Wilkes on September 1, 1936 in a wood frame house on the farm owned by maternal grandfather Arthur Wilmer Burch and grandmother Mary Jemima Foil Burch in the Mt. Pisgah Community. That house was torn down many years ago with the materials being used to build a newer home for Donnie and Sue Burch in the same location. A mantel from that tenant house was stored for years in the upstairs Burch log home until Daddy and Mother removed the mantel for Derry and me to use in our new home *Juanwood* named for our daughter Juanita. *Juanwood* was built in 1978 on 20 acres of the Dr. Ellis Estate on Highway 1053, Line Creek Road. We purchased the land from Emily Kent Owens, daughter of Dr. and Mrs. Ellis.

My parents, Earl and Willie, married October 6, 1934 at the Mt. Hermon Baptist Church Parsonage at Mt. Hermon, Louisiana. They had eight children: Bobbie Earl, Gwendora, Dorothy Elaine, (infant son who died at birth), Faye Ellen, Janice Marie, Kathy, and Earl Samuel "Chuck" Wilkes, Jr.

Parents Grew Cotton on Halves

Earl and Willie planted cotton on halves on the Burch land at the Mt. Pisgah crossroads when they lived in the Burch tenant house with Bobbie Earl (born January 15, 1935) and Gwendora (born September 1, 1936). They picked a bale of cotton every two and one-half days. Over a five day period, they picked two bales and took them to the cotton gin in Franklinton on Saturday. It took 1200 to 1400 pounds of lint cotton to make a bale. Two people picked 2400 to 2800 pounds of cotton within five days.

Mother shared with grandson Chris Wilkes how they had to walk in front of the Mt. Pisgah Baptist Church to get to their cotton field. Mother stated that the thing that hurt her and Daddy the most was taking Bobbie and me to the cotton field with them for the long days. They worried that a snake might come along or that bees might sting us while they were picking cotton on the far end of the field.

Mother shared with us a story of when she and Daddy were working in the field leaving Bobbie and me at the end of a row. I was in the baby buggy while Bobbie was a toddler around the age of 2 taking care of me. All of a sudden, Mother heard a loud scream and came running across the field finding me dirty and screaming from being flipped out of the buggy by Bobbie. Daddy told Mother that it was time for her to take us girls to the house, and she did.

Parents Became Sharecroppers

Daddy and Mother, along with daughters, Bobbie Earl and I, moved to a tenant house on the Gene Miller farm located approximately two miles from where Mother was born and raised. The Gene Miller farm was later owned by two of his daughters, the "old maids" Miss Mallie Miller and Miss Malvern Miller. Earl was a cotton sharecropper for the Miller sisters. Working as sharecroppers on the Miller farm, Daddy and Mother provided the labor, and the Miller sisters provided the plows, seed, mules, etc. with the harvest being split equally.

Two of the Wilkes children were born in this tenant house located where daughter Faye Ellen Wilkes built. They were Dorothy Elaine (born May 5, 1938) and Infant Son (born Dec. 23, 1940) who died at birth. One of my memories from living in this tenant house was a sweet potato bank that was a dugout in the ground where sweet potatoes were stored for the winter. When I was sent out to get some potatoes for cooking, I recall seeing the potatoes in the bank with a few sprouts. Perhaps, these sprouts were used for planting a new crop of sweet potatoes.

Because Daddy and Mother no longer lived near their "swimming hole" in the Dulaney Branch, Daddy hued from a large log a bath tub for bathing. They filled the tub in the morning with water drawn by hand from a well. During the day, the sun heated the water for them to bathe in the evening.

The "old maids" loved Daddy and Mother because of the improvements that they made on the farm. They loved Daddy because he worked every spare hour cleaning up the place: cutting briars, chopping down sassafras bushes, plowing, planting and gathering cotton and corn. The sassafras tree had an aromatic bark. I can remember picking up the roots found in a freshly plowed field and smelling the special root aroma. The dried root bark was used for flavoring and the source of a volatile oil. My parents boiled the root to make a tea for us. My sister Bobbie spilled a cup of this hot tea on her lower stomach area which caused a rupture.

The "old maids" showed their appreciation for Daddy and his work by bringing him cookies and coffee to the field. They were excellent cooks and knew that he loved their cooking.

Daddy and Mother worked a few years trying to make a living as sharecroppers. Mother plowed alongside Daddy as they planted, cultivated, and harvested cotton and corn. Daddy stated, "When you raise cotton, sometimes you make good cotton and sometimes you don't." He stated that he would get out in the winter and do public work, haul logs, or do something to feed his family through the winter. According to Daddy, the last cotton crop that he planted didn't make anything in the ten acre back field. He threw down his sack and crawled over the fence and went to hauling logs for "old man" Charlie Miller. He left Mother, Bobbie, and me to scrap up those little bolls of cotton.

Daddy bought an old Delta trailer that he could pull behind the old Chevrolet car that we had. He placed the trailer in the field so that Mother, Bobbie, Dorothy, and I wouldn't have to tote the cotton out of the field which was a long distance to the cotton shed near the house. Daddy cut through his field and hopped the fences to get on Mr. Charlie Miller's log truck by sun-up. He worked until after dark, depending on what time they got the logs to Bogalusa and got unloaded. Daddy came home after dark most of the time when logging. (Mr. Charlie Miller owned the farm adjoining the Wilkes farm.)

Parents Purchased the Miller Farm

At the end of three years, The Agricultural Adjustment program had begun. Daddy was determined to take advantage of this opportunity to buy a farm. The old maids' brother offered to rent the place from his sisters and then rent it to Daddy and Mother. Daddy told him that he wasn't going to rent anymore. Daddy was determined to buy him a place because he could buy a place, a plow or two, a mule and everything and start out on this rehabilitation program. Mr. Miller also offered to sell it to Daddy and Mother if they did not want to rent it. Mr. Miller learned of Daddy's determination to purchase a farm and did not want him to leave the "old maids" farm; therefore, they sold Daddy and Mother the place for a little of nothing. After selling the farm, the old maids built a white frame house on the Mt. Pisgah road near the Mt. Pisgah Baptist Church where they lived until their deaths.

Daddy and Mother purchased the house and 124 acres for $2500.00 on October 17, 1941. They paid the yearly note of $150.00 and 4% interest annually. (See property deed.) They moved from the tenant house into the big house on the Wilkes farm.

Faye Ellen was born (April 12, 1944) in the big house. Three of my siblings were delivered by Dr. Walter Crawford at the Walthall County Hospital in Tylertown, Miss. They were: Janice Marie (born September 29, 1946), Kathy (born September 25, 1951), and Earl Samuel Wilkes, Jr. (born January 27, 1953).

Medical Care Non-existent in the Rural Community

Times had really changed from the time that the older children were born at home with the only doctor in Mt. Hermon, coming to the house in his old raggedy car to deliver the babies and to the day that the younger ones were born in a hospital. There was no pre-natal care in the thirties. A woman could go see Dr. Brock at Mt. Hermon, if needed. (Willie and Earl have always believed that if their infant son had had the proper delivery care, he would have lived.)

Everyone in our community and in the surrounding communities was sent to the Charity Hospital in New Orleans, La. for any serious medical procedures. Sister Bobbie, at age six was playing with neighbors and sisters in the front yard of our home. We were all eating parched peanuts. While Bobbie was jumping rope, she sucked a peanut hull down her lung. Mother and Daddy took Bobbie to the Charity Hospital in N. O. with double pneumonia. She was examined by Dr. Hart who made several attempts to remove the peanut hull from her lungs. Bobbie recalls biting his fingers several times. Dr. Hart came out into the waiting area and told Mother and Bobbie that he could not remove the peanut hull, and there was nothing left to do. When he told Mother that nothing could be done, Bobbie remembers Mother crying. Bobbie reassured Mother, "I am going to be O.K." They were sent home for Bobbie to die. After being at home and a few days later, by some miracle, Bobbie coughed up the peanut hull. She fully recovered and is still going strong at age 78.

After Daddy and Mother had purchased the farm, they continued growing cotton and corn. Planting, growing, and harvesting corn produced feed for the animals and corn meal for the table. When it was time for Daddy to take corn to the grist mill in Clifton or Franklinton, La. for grinding into corn meal, he would have us girls go to the corn crib to shuck and shell the corn. There was always a fear of running into some mice while doing this chore.

After Daddy and Mother planted the corn, we girls helped thin the corn with a hoe. We also carried on our hips large buckets of soda while walking down the corn rows dropping the soda by the corn plants. When it was time to harvest the corn, usually in October during Fair time, we broke off the ears of corn, threw them in piles in a nearby row to be picked up later to be thrown onto the trailer and unloaded in the barn.

On one occasion during corn harvesting time, Daddy had promised that he and Mother would take us to the Fair if we finished gathering the corn. My sister Bobbie, one of the hardest working persons that I know, along with our sister Dorothy, and I worked very diligently to get the corn loaded onto the trailer.

Bobbie had worked so hard that she almost fainted and had to sit down for a few minutes. After we had completed loading the corn onto the trailer, we went to the house to get ready to go to the Washington Parish Fair. Much to our surprise and disappointment, the car had a flat tire which shattered our dream of going to the Washington Paris Free Fair that day.

Washington Parish "Free Fair"—Greatest Event of the Year

Growing up in this community and attending this Fair was the highlight of our year. Our parents grew up attending the Fair in their youth and knew how important the Fair was to us. The Washington Parish Free Fair was established in 1911 and is held the third week of October. It has been recognized as the largest parish/county Fair in the United States. This Fair was the largest yearly fun event for people in the Parish and surrounding communities without an admission charge.

Each year during the third week of October, for five days there is a steady stream of traffic coming into Franklinton or leaving Franklinton. People from South Mississippi and as far west as the Mississippi River and as far south as New Orleans make this pilgrimage each year. The Fair is still in existence and remains a "Free Fair" because local businessmen, citizens, and farmers refused to let it fade away. Some of the farmers in Washington Parish always depended on the fair to show off their wares, livestock and agriculture. The women used this opportunity to display their beautiful handmade quilts, household items, baked and canned goods, flower arrangements, art work, etc.

These people depended on this Fair as an outing to see old friends for the first time in a year. It was a time to socialize in a setting of several days of enjoyable entertainment for the entire family. There were trapeze artists performing on high wire, famous music performers, various country bands, and a rodeo. The midway and the Miles Branch Settlement attract the young and old. Students in the parish schools were very much involved in the activities at the Fair. I remember my second grade teacher had me prepare a penmanship paragraph for display in the schools building. Also, as a Home Economics ninth grader, I made and modeled a skirt and vest for competition, winning third place. For competition among schools in the Parish, FHA students entered baked, canned or sewn items; FFA students displayed their samples of vegetables and crops grown on the farms; and 4-H students brought all species of livestock for judging. During the early years, school buses throughout Washington Parish ran their school routes transporting students to and from the Fair.

My most exciting time at the Fair was in 1951 when I was sitting in the stands watching a livestock show when my friend and the love of my life, Derry Magee, crossed a creek and jumped over the benches to see me. He gave me a gift that he had just purchased while in Chicago, Illinois receiving the American Farmers Degree at the National FFA Convention. The gift was a heart-shaped gold compact with the FFA emblem on the front. That compact is in my collection of "personal treasures."

Upon learning that this year during the third week of October, 2011, the Washington Parish Free Fair would be celebrating its Centennial, Derry and I planned a trip back to Louisiana to attend the Fair. When my sister Janice Branch, who is on several Fair committees, asked me if I would be willing to ride in a surrey or buggy in the Fair Parade, I quickly accepted the invitation. I wore a Centennial outfit that I had used in Kentwood for its Centennial many years ago, borrowing a black skirt and black hat from my sister Bobbie Adams to complete the outfit. I rode with Mrs. Louquettie Burch, a 95 year-old family friend, who also wore a centennial dress and bonnet. She won the Promenade Contest on Thursday at the Fair wearing this beautiful dress and bonnet.

Everyone should take the opportunity to ride on some kind of float during the fair to see the magnitude of people lined up to watch the parade and to attend the Fair. There were working people, towns people, widows, widowers, rich, poor, office and store personnel standing in front of their businesses, professionals, special needs children and adults, nursing home people resting comfortably in their chairs covered with warm blankets, mentally and physically challenged people of all ages, people of all races, farmers, families, and hundreds of school children who were off from school the entire week for the Fair. Those attending and watching the parade were like one large family standing in the crowd waving and receiving candy that was thrown by the riders on the floats. Because this Fair has remained free from admission for 100 years, it allows all classes of people with little or no money to attend. I do have to say that it does cost parents a great deal of money if their children ride the rides, see the sideshows, purchase souvenirs, and buy food and snacks.

Dairying Replaced Cotton Farming

At some point, Daddy and Mother began a small dairy operation where they milked cows by hand until electricity came to the rural areas. At very early ages, all of their children served time in the dairy operation. We all learned to milk cows by hand in a nice dairy barn that had open windows which allowed air circulation for the cows, but it also allowed the cold winter wind to blow on us. We squeezed the cow teats, milking the milk into buckets that we held between our legs which allowed us to milk with both hands. We took the buckets of milk into a screened milk room, strained the milk into ten, eight, or five gallon cans, and had the cans ready to be picked up for hauling to the milk plant.

We mixed the cow feed in the feed room where the sacks of feed were delivered. At times, we used a shovel to mix cotton seed meal to the grain mixture. We poured buckets of feed into the cow stalls for them to eat while we were milking them. We also used a cane machete to cut sweet potatoes and turnips to supplement the cows' diet.

Sometimes, when we had a cow that wanted to kick while being milked, we hobbled her with a hobble designed to fit on the back of the cow legs restraining her from kicking. We also learned how not to get swished with a dirty wet cow tail. We tied a string around the cow's tail and then fastened it around her leg. We could milk and not be distracted by the swishing of a sometimes wet and dirty tail.

After we finished milking the cows, we turned them out into a pasture to graze during the day. We had to wash down the barn and back landing after each milking. We also had to wash and disinfect the milk pails and other utensils used in getting the milk transferred to the cans. After the cans were returned from the plant, we had to scrub and disinfect the milk cans to have ready for the next milking. This procedure was done twice a day seven days a week.

I have a memory of my father carrying by hand two five-gallon cans of milk, one by each hand, from the strainer room out to the milk shelf in front of the house and swinging them up on a high shelf for the milk hauler to pick up. The shelf was at the height of the truck body; therefore, the cans had to be swung from the ground onto the shelf. This required a strong back and strong muscles.

Earl Began Hauling Milk

Some years later, Mother and Daddy purchased a truck for Daddy to begin his first milk hauling route. He picked up five-gallon, eight-gallon, and ten-gallon cans of milk from the dairy farms on his route and carried them to the milk shed located in Mt. Hermon where the milk was dumped into large cooling tanks. The empty cans were washed and returned to the farms.

While school was in session, we had to get up early to go to the barn to milk and do the barn cleaning before going back to the house to eat breakfast and dress for school. We then had to walk ¾ of a mile to catch the school bus. In the late 1930's Washington St. Tammany Electric Coop (The REA) was formed, and it brought electricity to our community and our farm. At that time, we were able to switch from hand milking to machine milking. One of the nice things about having machines do the work, during the early morning milkings, we would go lie on a sack of feed in the feed room until it was time to transfer the electric milking machine to another cow. We also had to dip the teat cups in a disinfectant solution after the milking of each cow.

Electricity brought about many other conveniences to our farm and house. We had an electric pump for pumping water into the house. As we could afford it, electric appliances were added to our home such as: a refrigerator, a freezer, electric lights, and fans for cooling.

Milk processing improved over the years which required milk to be cooled immediately after the cow had been milked and the milk kept below 40 degrees Fahrenheit. This brought about a process where the cans of milk were placed in a cooler of ice water inside the strainer room in the barn. The hauler had to go into the strainer room on the farm to pull the cans of milk out of these coolers and swing them onto the truck. Bulk tanks eventually replaced the milk cans and Daddy replaced his can truck with a bulk tank truck. The trucks pumped the milk from the barn bulk tank into the bulk tank truck. The tank truck was an eighteen wheeler which held approximately 5,581 gallons of milk that were transported to a bottling plant, primarily in New Orleans, La.

When Daddy had to be away working other jobs, he did not have time to cultivate the corn. I was in school during the day, but I drove the tractor at night with Mother sitting on the seat next to me. We finished cultivating the corn by tractor light.

Silver Creek Was Center of Recreation

Daddy and Mother always rewarded us for our hard work by taking us to the Silver Creek which ran through my Grandfather Burch's land. Before we installed a bathroom in our house and many afternoons after milking, the family would drive to the creek with our soap, wash cloths, and towels to take our baths. During watermelon season, Daddy put watermelons in the creek to cool while we were swimming. Daddy also installed lights on a pole or in a tree so that we could swim at night. This creek was used for baptism by the Mt. Pisgah Baptist Church and other churches following a member's profession of faith in Jesus Christ. I, as well as my parents and some of my siblings, was baptized in this creek before churches installed baptistries.

Daddy Was an Excellent Sportsman

Fishing

Upon visiting my cousin, Robin Burch in 2011, he took us back on his land where he built a cabin near the bank of Silver Creek. In the bend of the Creek, there remains a deep hole which was named "The Tabby Hole" which has been there as long as anyone can remember. This hole had huge logs in the bottom providing a great place for these large catfish to live. "Uncle Dub" shared with Robin how he and his brothers and others used one of the old telephones to electrify the catfish in the bottom of this hole. As many as nine or ten catfish weighing between 40-50 pounds each surfaced the water and floated. The men excitedly gathered the fish that became fish for a family fish fry.

This method of "fishing" in the Silver Creek was recreation for all of the Burch sons, our father and his brother, community boys, other family members and friends. Some of the boys and men decided to have a contest to see who could "ring up" the largest catfish. Boys being boys, they decided to play a trick on the others. They inserted iron weights from old windows into the fish to add weight to their catch, but their unfair advantage was soon revealed.

I have a memory of Daddy and Uncle Dub and others pulling a large log out of the creek above the swimming hole where we all swam. They removed a large catfish from this log.

Daddy was a master fisherman. One afternoon, I accompanied Daddy with his rod and reel to the creek behind our farm to catch some trout. It was so exciting for me to see the trout swimming around in the creek, biting the bait, and becoming meat for our supper. Daddy, his father Lucion, family members, and friends set out trot lines on the Bogue Chitto River to catch fish for food. They caught some very large catfish which provided food for our family and enough fish for several fish fries.

At times, the "telephone" fishing method was used by several of these "fishers of fish" from the Mt. Pisgah community on the Bogue Chitto River, as well as, on Silver Creek. Robin has great memories of the pleasure he received from those fishing excursions with cousins behind the Wilkes farm on the Bogue Chitto River.

I have been told that because "telephone fishing" was illegal, the game warden tried every way he could to catch those participating in this sport but failed.

Hunting

Daddy was an excellent marksman as a hunter. He had excellent eyesight and only wore reading glasses during his older years. As a child, I remember seeing Daddy go down into the pasture with a carbide headlight at night to kill rabbits for meat. He hunted and killed squirrels and dressed them for mother to cook. She either fried or simmered them in a brown gravy to be eaten with hot biscuits. On one of his gaming excursions, he, Cleatus Cook, and Donnie Burch brought home an 8 foot 8 inch 250 pound alligator that they killed in the edge of the Bogue Chitto River and the dead creek behind our farm. On our farm during deer hunting season, he killed several deer with large racks. In fact, two of his mounted deer hang in our home office in College Station, TX.

Mother Was an Excellent Cook

On several occasions, Daddy took family and cousins camping on the banks of the Bogue Chitto River behind our farm. Mother was always supportive but chose to stay at the house and sleep in her bed at night. During skiing weather Daddy and the family met his brother, Willard Wilkes and his family, for weeks of camping at Percy Quin State Park in Mississippi. Mother would bake a large pan of chicken and dumplings and drive approximately 50 miles to bring it to the campers. Water skiing was a big part of our family's recreation at Percy Quin Lake and the Green's Lake near Franklinton.

Before Daddy and Mother were able to purchase a car, they traveled to church in a wagon pulled by a horse stopping along the way to pick up neighbors. Earl had a factory made seat with springs for the wagon while the rest of wagon owners had to sit on quilts or boxes. The back of the wagon would come out leaving an opening for the boys to sit on with their feet hanging down and dragging on the dirt road. The boys really liked riding this way.

In an oral history interview conducted by grandson, Christopher Wilkes, he asked Daddy and Mother what they did for entertainment during the Depression. Mother replied, "We did not have any. We just played with the children. The children would ride Daddy every night like a 'horsie.'" Willie stated, "This play was good for the children. It brought about a closeness with parents which you do not see today."

Chris asked Daddy if he had ever worked under any of FDR's programs. Daddy stated that he had worked with the WPA Program in the Mt. Pisgah area, digging dipping vats for the community cattle to be dipped for the fever tick. This WPA Program made jobs for the people to have jobs. Nearly everyone in the community worked in the program but would only get one or two days of work a week. This gave everybody a chance to work.

If there were a depression during my growing up years, I never knew it. I can remember when sugar was rationed, but we were never deprived because we had molasses as a substitute. Mother and Daddy made sure that we had everything that we needed to eat and to wear. During the war, people in the community brought scrap iron to the school yard to be shipped to factories to make weapons for the war. One day in the school yard, my sister Bobbie stepped on a piece of scrap wire which stuck in her foot. I have a vivid memory of our principal, Mr. Catha, a kind large man, picking Bobbie up in his arms and taking her into the school. Mr. C. B. Rogers, our Ag teacher, removed the wire from Bobbie's foot. The treatment at that time would have been to pour turpentine on the wound.

During the years Mother and Daddy were sharecroppers, they stated that they would get groceries and pay for them at the end of the year. They said, "It sounds like we were poor, but we weren't. We had everything that we needed and then some. We grew everything that we needed, even coffee. We didn't spend $50.00 the first year we were married. We even had the first indoor bathroom in the community!" Daddy told how he connected a car motor to a water tank and pumped water into the house.

I saw firsthand how cows left the farm to go graze in nearby wooded areas. Each herd of cows had a bell cow that led the way for the cows to and from the woods. The cow path is where the statement, "old cow syndrome" came from in referring to a person who never left a path to take advantage of new opportunities. It was always fun following the cow paths through the woods when we went berry picking. Of course, we always had to watch where we stepped to avoid the dung left by the cows.

One afternoon, my siblings and I went down into the woods to pick huckleberries. We found some bushes that were loaded with big blue berries. I was so excited and anxious to show Mother the berries that I had picked. I hurriedly rode the bike back to the house with the syrup bucket of berries hanging on the handle bars. As I rode the bike into the wash shed with the bike jumping onto the concrete landing, it jarred the berries out of the bucket. I was so disappointed that I had spilled the berries that were picked for Mother to make us a delicious blueberry pie or cobbler.

I experienced the process of syrup-making. Most of the early farmers grew sugar cane for making molasses or syrup. They carried the raw cane to a cane mill for cooking off the cane juice to make syrup. Daddy carried his sugar cane to Mr. Elton Miller's farm where his cane mill was located in our community. During syrup-making season, we passed by the mill each morning and afternoon in our grandfather Burch's school bus to and from school. Dorothy Elaine kept begging Uncle A.W. Burch (Uncle Dub as we called him), who was driving the bus, to stop at the cane mill to allow us to get a drink of cane juice. One day, he surprised us by taking the Alford bus riders home first and then stopping by Mr. Miller's cane mill for cane juice. This stop allowed Bobbie, Dorothy, and me to get a drink of cane juice.

The big yellow school bus owned by our grandfather, Arthur W. Burch Sr., continued to pick up students to transport them to and from the Mt. Hermon School at Mt. Hermon. Donnie, the youngest son and child began driving the school bus at age 14 due to the age of our grandfather, and the older brothers were away from home. The bus was driven by our younger uncle, Donnie Burch for most of his working life. His wife Sue continued driving the bus while Donnie worked for the Parish and State in road construction and maintenance until retirement. Economic times had improved allowing the bus drivers to drive to the houses of bus riders. Uncle Donnie drove to the front of the Wilkes house to pick up my younger siblings, Janice, Faye, Kathy, and Chuck. They did not have to walk that ¾ mile to catch the bus in the mornings nor walk home the ¾ mile in the afternoon.

Uncle Dub and Uncle Donnie Burch used the school bus for many purposes in transporting family members to and from town to purchase groceries and farm supplies. It transported people to ballgames, school events, each year for the fair, and was used for their personal transportation when dating, etc. Uncle A. W. and wife Mamie took a group of young people from Mt. Pisgah Baptist Church to Lake Ponchartrain for a day of swimming and picnicking.

One day, Uncle Dub drove the school bus to visit my parents at our home. While there, he decided that he would teach me how to drive. He drove the big yellow school bus in a pasture behind our house where he taught me how to shift, steer the bus, and drive in reverse. I was very happy to learn to drive and thought that I was ready to drive anything.

Neighbors Came for the "Hog Killing"

When it was time in the fall to kill hogs, several family members and neighbors gathered around to help with the "hog killing." This meant that a large barrel had to be buried slanted in

90

the ground and filled with boiling water heated in a large black iron pot by a fire. When the water temperature was appropriate, the hog was immersed in the barrel of water to loosen the hog's bristles and hair for easier scraping. Then the hog was cut into shanks of ham, sausages, and slabs of bacon and hung in the smokehouse to be hickory-smoked. A smoking fire had to be maintained day and night in the smokehouse with the salted meat being turned periodically. This hog-killing time was a time for sharing a "mess of meat" with our neighbors.

I can remember being a part of this process when the main activity for me was to help hold the sausage links as they came through the sausage grinder. The grinder ground the meat and filled the hog casings with seasoned sausage meat. These long lengths of sausage were hung over poles mounted in the smokehouse. The casing for the sausage required a very conscientious mother who meticulously cleaned the hog's intestines before filling them with the freshly ground sausage meat. I believe the standard procedure was to turn the intestine inside out to clean the intestines.

I observed my parents as they spent hours stirring and cooking in a large black iron pot, the cubes of fat and rind from the hog to make lard and cracklings. The lard was used for cooking and making soap. Before electricity came to our community, my mother had to build a fire in the cook stove early in the morning before preparing a meal. Each morning she made and cooked a pan of biscuits with some kind of smoked pork from the smokehouse. She fried fresh eggs from the chicken yard and at times made tomato gravy from freshly grown tomatoes or from a quart jar of canned tomatoes.

Tomato gravy became one of my daughter Nita's favorite breakfast foods. Molasses, cooked by Mr. Elton Miller at his cane mill, was always a part of our diet eaten on biscuits, corn bread, or used to make molasses cookies. I can still smell the aroma of molasses tea cakes as we entered the house after a day at school.

Mother cooked a complete lunch from the garden depending on what was in season at the time or foods that had been canned such as: peas, butterbeans, turnips, mustard greens, sweet and Irish potatoes, green beans, English peas, squash, etc. From a pen of farm raised chickens, Mother selected a chicken to be either fried or boiled for making a huge pan of chicken and dumplings, a family favorite to this day. She also made the best pan of chicken and dressing ever. I remember Daddy catching and dressing a large soft-shell turtle. Mother boiled the meat and used it like chicken in a delicious pot of dumplings.

Some of Mother and Daddy's daughters have perfected the making of chicken and dumplings and chicken and dressing. I made several attempts to make both but was never successful. In fact, my sisters asked me not to bring chicken/dressing to our family reunions. They would assign me something else to bring. Ha! Some of my siblings have carried on the chicken and dumplings tradition which is a favorite for their families and at church dinners.

Mother Spent Hours Cooking in the Kitchen

If there were not enough leftovers for supper, Mother would cook the evening meal on the wood stove. After a hard day working outside and for a quick supper, Mother would bake a huge pone of cornbread for us to eat in a bowl of milk. Cold baked sweet potatoes were always a good snack after school and were good eaten in a bowl of milk in the evening. During the cold months, Daddy built fires in the fireplaces in the living room, bedroom, and kitchen. Using these fireplaces called for several cords of firewood during the year. It was our duty to bring in the wood for the stove and the fireplaces.

During this time, there was no running water in the house. Water was drawn by hand from the well using a long slender tin bucket. Fresh water was drawn daily and placed on the water shelf on the back porch for drinking and washing hands and face in preparation to eat after a time of working outside. There was a large white sack cloth hanging on a nail next to the shelf for drying hands and face. Water also had to be drawn for cooking, washing dishes, and washing clothes.

Washing Clothes by Hand Was an All Day Job

The washing of clothes was done under the wash shed next to the smoke house. We used two No. 3 tin wash tubs, one for the washing and the other for rinsing the clothes. Clothes were pinned by clothes pins to wires that were attached to two poles in the yard for drying clothes. A fire was used to heat the water in the big black iron pot for cleaning overalls and other deeply soiled items. Mother used a large hickory paddle to move the clothing around in the hot soapy water to remove the dirt from the overalls. Washing was only done on sunny days so that the laundry could dry.

Water was brought into the pantry from the porch, through the dining room and kitchen where the dishwashing took place. Water was heated on the stove for dishwashing. Following the washing and rinsing of dishes, the water had to be discarded. Due to the distance young girls had to carry dish pans of soapy dirty water to empty the water, we decided that it would be easier just to dump the pans of water out through the screened window in the pantry. Of course, Daddy had to replace the screen several times due to the lye soap eating holes in the screen. This soapy water kept the wisteria vine growing profusely and helped keep the fig tree watered and fed.

I Suppose We Had Some Sibling Rivalry

Sister Dorothy Elaine, as a younger sibling in the house observing what was going on, remembered this story. One day during dishwashing time, our sister Bobbie became frustrated with me because evidently, I was not helping with the dishwashing chores. She left the kitchen and dining room area to tell mother that I was not helping. Upon Bobbie's return to the kitchen, I was hiding behind the dining room door with a large spoon. As she passed by the dining room door, I hit her in the top of the head causing her eyes to roll back. Her body buckled, and she fell to the floor. There is no recollection of Mother applying any consequences for my behavior, but it is assumed that Mother had us hug and make up. If Mother ever used any physical punishment, it was with a tiny bridal wreath stem that would only sting the naked legs. She and Daddy never allowed us to fuss or fight.

Another fun incident that we remember was when Daddy was trying to find out who had stuck a finger in the butter. He made quite a production out of it as he continued to question each one of us. Neither of us ever admitted to sticking our finger in the butter, and to this day, we are not sure who did. Elaine, being the youngest, stated that if she did it she does not remember doing it.

House Cleaning Was Different in This Day

During spring cleaning time, the four cotton mattresses from the three bedrooms were brought to the front porch on a hot sunny day to make them fluffy and clean. The springs were taken out and washed. When it was time to clean the heart pine floors, they were scrubbed with a homemade shuck scrub brush. Scrubbing those pine floors required much elbow grease. Mother would come through the hallway to check to see if the floors were clean. She said that the floors were not clean until she could smell the pine.

Mother swept the pine wood floors with a sage brush broom that she and Daddy made. When the sage brush broom was worn out, Mother would go to the fence row and cut some more sage brush to make a new broom. She bundled together the sage brush and wrapped a cord around them to hold them together.

Homemade Clothes a Necessity

Cow feed was delivered to us in floral printed cotton sacks that were used to make dresses, panties, shorts, and window curtains. One of our favorite memories was seeing Daddy sitting on the floor cutting out panties from the sacks and then watching him sew them on the treadle sewing machine. Mother used the sack fabric to make ruffled curtains that covered the four windows in the front bedroom. This sewing required hours of peddling by foot on the treadle sewing machine to stitch the seams. As time progressed, Mother was able to go to town to buy the cloth to make our dresses for school.

On one of her rare trips away from the house to go to town, she left us at the house by ourselves. I wanted to try my hand at cutting hair, so Dorothy Elaine became the victim. I began cutting her beautiful dark thick hair so that she would have bangs. The longer I tried to straighten the bangs, the shorter the bangs became. I stopped cutting when I had created a V-shape in the bangs, and there was no more to be cut. Upon Mother's return, we found Dorothy hiding under the bed. When she came out, she stated, "Me little Beaver." Even though it took a while for the hair to grow out, it did grow back and was as pretty as ever.

Because Bobbie and I had to walk quite a distance to catch our grandfather's school bus in the morning, I was concerned that sister Dorothy Elaine who was beginning her first year of school would not be able to walk the distance. I told her that if she got tired I would carry her. This was an example of how much love and compassion we had for each other. There would not have been any way for me to carry her since I was only two years older than she. But, it was the thought that counted.

Bobbie, Elaine and I were each given a Holstein calf to personally bottle feed and water. We had become very attached to them and were so proud of our beautiful calves. One night, the calves happened to get out of the pasture, found their way to an open bucket of soda in the tool shed and ate it. The next morning we found our calves stretched out and stiff. Loosing these calves was one of the saddest experiences of our young lives.

Daddy Never Allowed "Giving Up"

Daddy was able to purchase a new Farmall Super A tractor that was used for planting corn and a large garden, cultivating the corn and garden, clipping pastures, and mowing the large stomp.

I was always following Daddy wherever he was working on the farm. It became imperative that we girls learn to drive the tractor since Daddy did not have a son at that time. Daddy always encouraged us to do things that we might not have thought that we could do. When Daddy brought home our first bicycle, he took us and the bicycle out to the road in front of our house. After a weak attempt to ride, Daddy put me on the bicycle and pushed me as hard and as fast as he could. I could do nothing but ride the bike. We had similar experiences when we needed to learn how to swim. If we were not making the proper amount of progress, he would throw us into the creek and make us swim. Daddy was not cruel in any way. He just pushed us so that we would not allow fear to keep us from accomplishing things.

The time came for Bobbie and me to learn to drive the new Farmall Super A tractor. We were to drive the tractor and trailer around to the back of the dairy barn. Reluctantly, Bobbie sat in the driver's seat, and I rode on the draw bar standing behind her. She had the tractor in the lowest gear possible, and we were barely moving taking the tractor and trailer behind the dairy barn. The left front tractor tire crossed over a piece of concrete in the ground which caused the tires to go to the left. The tractor continued traveling in that diverted path right into a cable guide wire which was helping to support an electric light pole. A bolt on the tractor muffler caught on the cable wire, and the tractor gradually climbed the wire as far as the tractor would go. The tractor choked down as it was suspended in the air and being held by the bolt on the muffler. Bobbie remained in the driver's seat holding onto the steering wheel, and I was still holding onto the seat behind Bobbie. We did not panic! We just rode the tractor up the guide wire. Daddy

96

calmly came to our rescue. He placed a large empty oil or gasoline barrel on the ground under the tractor. He used a thick creosote timber on top of the barrel to allow the tractor to roll down the timber to the ground. Could it have been that we were not old and not mature enough to take on this responsibility? Evidently not! Daddy did not think so! He had all of the confidence in the world in us.

On one occasion, our family, Daddy, Mother, Bobbie, Elaine and I excitedly gathered together on the edge of the field near the gate that led to a path to the Bogue Chitto River. Daddy wanted to begin clearing out some trees to build a camp. I had become the "experienced" tractor driver, so Daddy had me get on the Farmall Super A and back down to a small tree that we were going to pull up. For some reason, I put my foot on the clutch and caused the tractor to fly down this bluff. I heard Daddy hollering, "Release the clutch!" It was too late! By some act of God, as I was flying down the bluff, the two front tires turned sideways and caught against a tree. This stopped the tractor and allowed me to get off. I was amazed as I walked up the bluff that my head scarf was still in place that covered my hair rolled and held by bobby pins in preparation for a date that evening. Mother and my siblings witnessed this event and reported that Daddy flew between two trees trying to get to me. They went back later to see where the incident occurred and saw that there was no humanly way possible for Daddy to have gone between those two trees. But, he evidently did because he had several witnesses to prove that he did. This ended the clearing of the land to build a camp.

Immediately following this tractor episode, J. L. "Nook" Miller drove up on his bicycle delivering the *Grits* newspaper wanting to know what had happened. Had he been a writer for the paper, he could have had written an interesting story on the spot.

If the family did not have a car or truck available, we would hook the tractor to a trailer and travel to a neighbor or family member's house. During fruit gathering season, Mother decided to take us to Malcolm and Exie Miller's farm adjacent to our farm to pick some fruit. The tractor was hooked to the hitch on the four-wheel wagon by a bolt or pin. Mother was driving the tractor with us children sitting on the bed of the trailer. As she was going up the hill, she shifted gears, causing the pin to come out of the hitch and allowing the trailer to roll back down the hill and into the red clay embankment, jostling us around on the trailer. Faye's foot was injured on the top and side, causing it to bleed profusely. We do not know who got us out of this predicament, and we cannot remember if we continued our trip to the neighbor's house that day or not. But, we survived another tractor accident. It seemed as though God was always protecting us.

Growing up in this community provided me an opportunity at an early age to see and experience my parents' and grandparents' way of supporting each other, the church, family, and community members. They were always supportive of the ministers and their work at Mt. Pisgah Baptist Church and in the surrounding communities. Daddy never served as a deacon nor Bible teacher at church, but he certainly served the church and community in ways that demonstrated his faith in God.

One example of community service involved Leon Schilling who was bedridden during his last years. He was a tenant farmer on M. John Alford's and Claudie Bankston's farms. (John's wife, Mary Burch, was my great aunt and Claudie's wife, Louvenia Wilkes, was also my great aunt.) Each year the Mt. Pisgah Community got together and planted, cultivated, and gathered a crop for Leon. I have a memory of being at Leon's house one night when he was breathing so hard that we could hear him outside in the yard. The community people were there to be with him and the family during his last hours.

During the late 1930's and early 1940's when the farmers had little cash, a church storehouse was built so that farmers could bring part of their crops at harvest time as their tithe. Every tenth load of corn, gallon of syrup, etc. was considered their tithe. The produce was sold and monies received were used in the operation of the church. Any money that the Mt. Pisgah Church received, one tenth was given to the Cooperative Program, a practice that has continued to this day. Tithing was an important practice for my parents, Derry's parents, and for Derry and me as Christians.

Daddy was referred to as a "jack of all trades." He was an excellent mechanic, electrician, carpenter, builder, plumber, and machine repairman. His mother, Lavanda, stated that Earl would take apart any piece of machinery or equipment to see how it was made. Perhaps that is one way he learned to be so proficient at many trades. He was always involved in helping with church construction projects. After electricity came to the community, he wired houses for neighbors. He always readily received discarded lawn mowers, clothes dryers, washing machines, motors of all kinds, and various pieces of farm equipment to repair and pass on to one of his children, grandchildren, or neighbors who could use them.

Always Showing Christian Hospitality

Mother and Daddy were good examples of showing Christian hospitality to family, friends, neighbors, and, especially ministers. Bro. Harold Anderson served two churches part-time at the same time, Mt. Pisgah and Mt. Hermon. He always found the Wilkes home to be a great place to sleep and eat when he was on the church field or in the surrounding communities.

Derry's father, Rev. Marvin Magee, pastor at Mt. Hermon Baptist and Rev. Earnest Dearman, pastor at Kentwood Baptist Church, squirrel hunted and fished with Daddy. They loved coming to the Wilkes home for the fellowship and good hospitality. My Mother, "Miss Willie," always had plenty of good food cooked. Bro. and Mrs. Magee became good friends with Daddy and Mother after Derry and I married.

On one occasion, Bro. Magee and Daddy decided that they would like to barbeque a goat. They acquired a goat and skinned it by making certain no goat hair touched the meat. After they finished preparing the meat for barbequing, Daddy tacked the goat hide to dry on the wall of the tool shed in between the pastures and the milk barn. At milking time, we drove the cows from the pastures for milking. Just before the cows reached the shed, they all scattered in all directions and could not be driven to the milk barn. Many attempts were made to get the cows to follow the path that they had always followed to the barn. Daddy even engaged horse riders in an attempt to get the cows past this shed. It finally dawned on Daddy that the only difference in the situation was the goat hide hanging on the shed wall. The smell of the goat hide frightened the cows so that they would not come near the shed. When Daddy removed the hide, the cows finally cooperated by coming into the milking barn lot to be milked. This was a hard lesson learned. Daddy and Bro. Magee did barbeque the goat. Daddy insisted that all of the children try eating it, but some refused to partake.

Dr. Nelson Price, pastor of the Mt. Pisgah Baptist Church, was another pastor who made his home away from home at the Earl Wilkes farm. Nelson was an outstanding basketball player at Southeastern Louisiana University while in college there. He spent many hours at the Wilkes house playing basketball with Dorothy, Faye, and Janice out by the tool shed. Daddy nailed a rim from a wooden keg to the boards on the tool shed that was to the left of the front yard. This is where the Wilkes girls learned how to shoot and play guard, becoming excellent basketball players.

Daddy later built a basketball goal near the edge of the front porch and next to the pump house where the girls, other family members, and visitors spent hours shooting and playing basketball. The ball goal and backstop remain in this location today at the Wilkes house. After Derry and I and Bobbie and Quinlon were married and came home to visit, Derry and Quinlon played basketball in this area. Faye and Janice got a lot of practice trying to shoot over these two TALL brothers-in-law. Perhaps, that was one of the reasons why Janice became a state basketball forward champion on the basketball court and Faye an All State Guard in 1962.

The Wilkes home was the gathering place for their children, grandchildren, and great-grandchildren on holidays and other times when they just dropped in for a visit. Daddy hung an automobile tire swing in a pecan tree outside their home many years ago. The Wilkes grandchildren enjoyed many hours swinging on the swing over the years. Their great-grandchildren have also enjoyed the swing. When our parents were no longer living in the home, we took our grandchildren there specifically to have the experience of swinging. One of the summers that our grandson Ross from Miami, FL, spent the summer with us in College Station, Texas, we took him to the Wilkes place to play. He enjoyed, not only swinging on the tire swing, but a ride in Aunt Faye's go cart up and down the road from my niece, Tam Brooks' house to pick blueberries and back to Aunt Faye's for a bicycle tire repair.

Serving Their Church and Community

Daddy and Mother were always involved in various projects at their church. When Bro. Bill Quartrone came to Mt. Pisgah as their pastor, he had a construction/building background. He used his own money to purchase a large portable classroom building from the Washington Parish School Board for Sunday School classrooms at Mt. Pisgah. Daddy helped Bill and others move the building onto the Mt Pisgah Church property where it is now used as educational space. Bro. Bill also engaged several church members in helping make home repairs for members in the community. Sister Janice and Mother became involved in helping to decorate the church parsonage that was remodeled at that time.

Daddy and Mother were very best friends with "Uncle Joe" and "Miss Quettie" Burch, as we called them. Joe was mother's first cousin who shared the same great-grandfather, John R. Burch, Sr. and the same grandfather, John R. Burch, Jr., as my mother and her siblings. My parents, Uncle Joe and Miss Quettie, became convicted that something needed to be done about the Burch Cemetery which had been neglected for many years.

While Derry and I were living in Kentwood, we remembered hearing Mother and Daddy tell how they, along with Uncle Joe and Miss Quettie, had worked in honoring their forefathers in cleaning the gravesites in this Cemetery. With the help of other family members, they cleaned out the underbrush, trimmed trees, and cut grass around the tombstones. Great-Grandson Donald "Donnie" Burch, sometimes with the help of descendants of other families who were buried there, helped maintain this Burch Cemetery as long as he lived. Today, at age 95, Miss Quettie engages the help of Uncle Donnie's three sons to help maintain the Burch Cemetery.

After Derry and I began our genealogical journey, we visited the Burch Cemetery with Miss Quettie. Derry and I returned the next day with our cleaning products and brushes to help Miss Quettie, Donnie's son Sherman, and a descendant of another family to clean the tombstones and pull up small trees and bushes growing in the tombs. We were very puzzled as to why John R. Burch, Sr. does not have a grave marker. According to publications and cemetery records, our great-great-grandfather, John R. Burch, Sr., is buried in an unmarked grave next to his wife, Samantha Clowers Lewis. John and Samantha had two children (John R. Burch, Jr. and ? Nancy Burch?). After John R. Burch, Sr. died, his wife Samantha Clowers married four other times. She married Thomas Bickham (1795-1838) who was the son of Abner Bickham (1755-1834). They had two children (Abner Clower Bickham and ...?) After Thomas' death, she married Isaac A. Myles. They had at least two children (Ed Myles and Rebecca Myles). The name of her fourth husband was Coleman Holmes (whom she divorced). She married her fifth and last husband, William Lewis, in 1860. She outlived her last husband by 14 years; he died in 1874, she in 1891 at age 80. Evidently, her Lewis children buried her and built the brick tomb which was at one time covered with a marble slab. The slab has been removed and has left only the several layers of bricks on her grave. I still cannot understand why Richard Burch, Sr. does not have a marker on his grave. There is a large sandstone at the foot of what appears to be his grave next to Samantha's grave. The cemetery and historical records state that he was buried next to

Samantha. It would be better stated that Samantha was buried next to him since she was buried last.

Since William Lewis was Samantha's fifth and last husband, this might explain why her tombstone in the Burch Cemetery reads, "Samantha Lewis."

MY PARENTS

Earl Samuel Wilkes, Sr. and Willie Marie Burch Wilkes

Daddy's History

Earl Samuel Wilkes, Sr. (1912-1994) was born on February 5, 1912 in Clifton, Louisiana, located in Washington Parish, La. to Lucion Wilkes (1884-1952) and Lavanda Armentha Morris (1890-1971). He was the third of nine children.

On October 6, 1934, Earl married Willie Marie Burch at the Mt. Hermon Baptist Church parsonage. Willie was born on January 30, 1915 to Arthur Wilmer Burch (1873 —1948) and Mary Jemima Foil Burch (1883-1971).

Earl's family are descendants of Thomas Wilkes of Edgecombe County, North Carolina. (*History of Genealogy of Thomas Wilkes*, 1965.) The Wilkes family migrated from North Carolina through South Carolina, Alabama, and Mississippi. Eventually, the Wilkes family came to Louisiana when Earl's great-grandparents, John Brown Wilkes (1819-1860) and Oney Rebecca Pritchard Wilkes (1823-1858) moved to Claiborne Parish, Louisiana, settling about five miles south of Homer, La. where he farmed.

Due to the serious illness of both John Brown Wilkes and Oney Rebecca Pritchard Wilkes, they sold their property in Louisiana in 1856-1858 and invested the proceeds in cash and divided their slaves among their children who were placed with relatives. Earl's grandfather, Samuel Warren "Sam" Wilkes, was sent to live with Liberty and Rebecca Warren of Marion County, Mississippi. "Sam" Wilkes (1849-1918) was one of the early boatmen of Pearl River.

In 1896, Samuel built a boat known as the 'Carrie B.' which he owned with Hubert and Hilton Bailey. He made many trips between New Orleans, La. and Columbia, Mississippi, and on occasion of very high water, the boat went as far up the river as Monticello and old Westville. The main cargo was cotton to New Orleans and general merchandise out of New Orleans to the towns along the river. The competition of the railroad eventually put the river boats out of service. Also, the boats were unable to keep a regular schedule, as they could not navigate the Pearl except when it was "up" from heavy rains causing their service to be unreliable.

After his steamboat days, Samuel Warren Wilkes, Sr. married Vandellia Dorcas McMillan of Angie, Louisiana. After their marriage, they lived for a while in Angie and in 1875 moved to St. Francisville, Louisiana, where they lived on the Fairview Plantation for several years before moving back to Angie. They had twelve children.

Earl's father, Lucion Wilkes, seventh child of his parents, was born in St. Francisville, La. where he was educated by a private tutor and studied French, as one of his subjects in the public schools. Lucion, as a single man, came to live with his sister, Louvenia and husband Claudius Bankston whose farm was located on the corner of Highway 38E and Mt. Pisgah Road. Earl stated, *Papa came over here, and that's where he ran up on Mother and married her.* Earl's mother Lavanda was raised at Mt. Hermon on the old James Washington Morris home place which is still owned by some Morris family members.

Earl recalled that his family came from North Carolina, settled in Bogalusa, and moved out to Angie and gradually shifted to the Mt. Hermon community. His parents, Lucion and Lavanda moved around but remained in various locations in the Mt. Hermon Community.

Earl and his siblings attended school at Bogue Chitto through the sixth or seventh grade and transferred to Mt. Hermon High School where he graduated. Earl and Willie Marie Burch met at Mt. Pisgah Baptist Church and Mt. Hermon High School. Earl stated, *Oh, I was floating around. I would go here and yonder. Finally, I settled down and started going to Mt. Pisgah. We had met going to school together, so I just got to hanging out in Mt. Pisgah, and that's where I wound up.* (Our brother, Chuck Wilkes, has a church bench from the Mt. Pisgah church that has the initials E.W. and W.B. carved on the back by Earl when they were attending church as a couple.)

After Earl graduated high school in 1933 which was the middle of the Depression, he went to Shreveport, La. for two years to help build roads. Earl and Willie wrote each other every day. They dated four years before marrying. Earl couldn't settle down because he had to follow his job, making a living. He was also waiting for Willie to finish school before they married. Earl began working on the roads near Shreveport, La., making $.25 an hour.

After some time, they gave Earl a tractor driving job pulling brooms and things which increased his pay to $.35 an hour. While working on the roads, he did anything by hand, riding a tractor, shoveling dirt and anything that needed to be done. Earl

106

stated, "If the foreman told you to get it, you got it." Before he left Alexandria, he was keeping up the boss's car. The boss would take him with him and put him in the car to drive. If the boss got out to check the road, he wanted that car to be right there (maybe ¼ mile) from him when he got ready to get in. Earl was still getting $.35 per hour to chauffer the boss around.

Earl and Willie Marie Burch, daughter and sixth child of Arthur Wilson Burch and Mary Jemima Foil Burch, were married on October 4, 1934 at the Mt. Hermon Baptist Church parsonage. They had eight children: Bobbie Earl, Gwendora, Dorothy Elaine, deceased infant son, Faye Ellen, Janice Marie, Kathy, and Earl Samuel, Jr.

Mother's History

Our mother, Willie Marie Burch, was born January 30, 1915 in a house that was built for her parents, Arthur Wilmer Burch (1971-1948) and Mary Jemima Foil Burch (1883-1971 by Arthur's father, John R. Burch, Jr. The house was built on a hill directly across from the Burch Cemetery on the Mt. Pisgah Road where the Donnie Burch home is today. Earl and Willie grew cotton on halves with Willie's parents. There was a swimming hole in the creek on the Burch farm behind the church where Earl and Willie took their baths during the summer after picking cotton. When they returned home, they pulled their mattresses outside to sleep on because the weather was so hot. This swimming hole is still there and is referred to as "Earl and Willie's swimming hole."

Willie's grandfather John Burch, Jr. gave all of his children 60 acres of land each. Arthur started out with 60 acres and bought other land from siblings –Weston Burch was one part that he purchased.

The Burch land was homesteaded by Arthur's father, John Richard Burch, Jr. who was the son of John Richard Burch, Sr., and a grandson of Richard Burch who came from Georgia and settled the Richard Burch Headright in the Mt. Pisgah Community. He later acquired two other Headrights in the general area. (See the Era-Leader newspaper article which is attached to this history on John R. Burch, Jr. who fought in the Civil War.)

John Richard Burch, Jr. — a Prosperous Farmer

After the Civil War, John Richard Burch, Jr. became a prosperous farmer and large landowner in the Mt. Pisgah Community. John owned a section of land (640 acres), extending from Highway 1056 past the Silver Creek area and all of the land across the Mt. Pisgah Road in front of the church all the way down to where A. W. Burch, Jr. lived.

John built a house for Arthur and Jemima on a hill facing the Mt. Pisgah Road. Earl and Willie lived in the house for approximately three years, raising cotton on halves for Arthur and Jemima. Bobbie Earl and I were born in this house.

John R. Burch, Jr. built the two-story log house on his land where his eleven children were raised. Later Arthur and Jemima acquired the two-story log house built by his father, John R. Burch, Jr. They raised their ten children on this Burch Estate and lived there until their deaths. (All of the Wilkes children have a picture of this house that was photographed by Wilson Burch's son, Edward Burch.)

Willie stated that her Grandpa John R. Burch Jr. built this two-story house of split logs. Earl responded, *It wasn't built of split logs but built of round logs with both sides being faced with molds which gave two finished sides. They done a lot of hueing to hue those things out. They moraced them at the end, just like that, and stacked them up and went right on up with that thing. And there are sills under that house, Oh! My God! There are some of them sills that big around (spreads arms in a large circle). Just floor joists, you know, they had them heart timbers that John pulled up there.* Sadly, this house was set fire several years ago by arsonists and completely burned. Willie regrets that the old piano had never been removed from the house and restored before the fire.

Mother grew up with loving parents and grandparents who were very successful farmers and businessmen. Her grandfather, John Richard Burch, Jr., donated the land for the Burch Cemetery where he and wife Melissa Brumfield are buried. This Cemetery is about ¼ mile from the Mt. Pisgah Baptist Church and across the road from the Burch estate. In the late 1880's or 1890's Mother's father, Arthur Burch, donated the land for the Mt. Pisgah Baptist Church Cemetery where he and Jemima are buried. Mother and Daddy and two of their children are buried in this church Cemetery.

Arthur and Jemima reached success in all of their farming and business operations. Mother always talked about how sweet and gentle her father was. She also talked about how hard her mother worked. Mother's parents with the help of all their children worked very diligently to purchase the large section of Burch land. They grew cotton; grew corn and other crops for the mules, pigs, and cattle; ran a dairy farm; hauled milk to Clifton and Kentwood; raised and sold vegetables and beef to the public; and operated a school bus route from the Burch home to Mt. Hermon High School for over 50 years.

Arthur was one of the few farmers in the community who had a dairy. Dairying was the main source of income and is what kept them going. Willie remarked, *how the other people made it, I don't know.* Earl stated that Arthur was one of the first dairymen in this area, along with *old man Ab Miller.* Arthur milked cows by kerosene light. Mr. Porter carried the milk to Clifton, Louisiana. A train called *The Doddlebug* carried it on to New Orleans. Willie commented that her father and other farmers took turns carrying the milk to Bogalusa (30 miles from the Burch farm) to meet the train to load the five gallon or eight gallon cans of milk to be shipped to New Orleans. Earl stated that they went through the Enon route to meet the train that came through Bogalusa and loaded the cans of milk to be shipped to New Orleans. Earl commented, *I don't know how they ever got the cans back...but, that's the way the milk got to New Orleans.*

At some later point, the dairy farmers in the area, Arthur Burch, Mr. Porter, Mr. Ab Miller, and Wilson Smith carried milk to Clifton and Kentwood to meet the trains going to New Orleans. Later Arthur trucked his milk to Kentwood, La. in the back of an old Ford touring car in which he took out the back seat. The car had a dished shaped area under it, and Arthur floored it to make a flat area for transporting the milk cans. Earl recalled that there were many old Ford cars around the community at that time —old man Bertie Alford had a Chevrolet.

Arthur and Jemima had hogs that ate the branches by the creek during the day and came back to the house at night for the corn that they feed them. They butchered the hogs and cows for meat. People came to their house on Saturday to buy the meat out of a big washtub. During the spring and summer, they took vegetables to Franklinton to sell and returned with ice that they had purchased. They buried the ice in cottonseed to keep it cold until they arrived home to put it in an icebox.

In an interview, grandson Chris Wilkes asked Earl and Willie if her parents had a car before they were married. Earl replied, *yeah, they did, 'cause we went to the ball games in it when Milford was living, I mean, when he was around there. The car stayed down there in that old shed at the Burch farm. It was a model-a shut-in they called it. He got a model A when they came out, and he got one that was all glassed in—had doors with glass windows that let up. They called it a glass 'shut-in.' They gave them all kinds of names back then.*

Grandmother Jemima was an excellent cook and homemaker. She was gifted playing the piano and could play any tune on the piano that she knew. Our mother also had this gift of playing by ear and could play anything on the piano that we requested. We could hum Mother a tune, and she would make the *piano roll*. One of our favorite songs for her to play was *Down Yonder*. Every Sunday after church, there was a large group of young people who came home with the Burch children for Sunday dinner. Grandmother's house was always open to anyone who needed a place to eat or stay. It was truly a house of hospitality! Grandmother Burch became mentally disabled in 1929 approximately five years after Dorman was born. She seemed to recover for a time and later became pregnant with Donald John. After Donald John was born, she remained in this disabling mental condition until her death in 1971 and could still play the piano as she always had. The youngest daughter dropped out of school in the eighth grade and spent the remainder of her life helping to take care of her father, mother, and siblings.

Grandmother lived to be 88 years old and Grandfather Burch lived to be 75 years old. He died of cirrhosis of the liver.

Sister Bobbie and I have vivid memories of Grandfather Burch walking with a whiskey bottle in his pocket with his hands behind his back. On one occasion, I accompanied my mother on the 1 ½ mile walk from the Wilkes home to the Burch home to help sober Grandfather who was slumped down on the front porch. Mother helped her sibling move him onto the porch swing. At this point, I saw what alcohol could do to a person and a family. This experience made an indelible impression on me and gave me the fortitude to never allow alcohol to enter my body nor my home. I have always stated that if my child, grandchildren, or other family members chose to consume alcohol, it would never be because of my influence.

A grandson who owns a part of the Burch estate tells how many whiskey bottles were found under the roots of a tree that he cut down. Evidently, this was where Grandfather stashed his whiskey or the place where he kept bottles for storing his moonshine that he made for his personal consumption. My cousin, Robin Burch, who inherited some of the Burch land from his father, Donnie Burch, took us on his property in November, 2010 and showed us the location where Granddaddy Burch made his whiskey. Many years ago Aunt Vivian showed Robin where the still was located. Granddaddy evidently used a spring for his water source because the still was located several hundred feet from Silver Creek which runs through his land.

In August, while Derry and I were visiting my sisters at Mt. Pisgah, Robin gave us permission to come and dig for whiskey bottles. Derry, sisters Bobbie and Dorothy, and I took our shovels and spent a couple of hours digging for bottles. We found four and decided that we had enough. We have an open invitation to come back to dig.

Looking back and thinking about what an adjustment the family must have had to make when grandmother became disabled in the midst of raising ten children. It is amazing that the Burch children had such a good sense of humor and good outlook on life. One of my mother's saddest memories was when she and her siblings visited Grandmother in the Mental Hospital in

Jackson, La. The lives of these family members could have been very different had they had the medicine and medical support that people have today who have mental or emotional difficulties.

Two of Mother's sisters had to return to the home to live due to health conditions and unsuccessful marriages. One aunt suffered severe spousal abuse which caused her to be disabled the remainder of her life. The other sister was crippled from flebitis that developed from a briar scratch. The two aunts later went to nursing homes near their grown children. The unmarried sister who had spent her life caring for the family at the Burch home died in a nursing home.

Our Super Mom

Our Mother, Willie Marie Burch Wilkes, was a "Super Mom." She not only raised seven children, made their clothes, cooked three meals a day, took care of the house, and helped Daddy on the farm, but she helped take care of her parents and younger siblings at the Burch home. Each year Mother and Daddy helped plant a vegetable garden at the Burch home for the sisters and Grandmother after the some of the Burch boys had all married and moved away. Mother shopped for clothes and groceries for her mother and sisters. Mother was their bookkeeper and advocate for their financial needs for many years. She took care of their personal and medical needs. She also helped the family maintain the home.

Daddy, a handyman who could fix anything, helped make repairs to the house when needed. Our daughter, Juanita, as a little girl, recalled accompanying Mother to the Burch home where Mother swept and dusted the beautiful pine board walls. Mother loved the Burch home where she was born and raised. It was such a part of her and her family. She lived the remainder of her life with Daddy at the Wilkes farm which was only 1 1/2 miles from her childhood home. She lived to be 87 years old and never lived farther than the 1 ½ miles from where she was born.

Because of her love for the Burch home and its furnishings, Mother removed the Victorian furniture from the living room at the home in fear of someone breaking in and stealing these family treasures. She later gave the settee, two straight chairs, and a large chair and rocker to me. She knew that I had always treasured antiques, family furniture, and relics of the past. She later removed the oak armoire from the house and gave it to me. Derry and I had glass doors and shelves installed as it was being refinished. It is used as a China cabinet in our dining room.

Willie and her siblings walked a long cow path through the woods crossing the Dulaney Branch to attend grammar school at Mt. Ebal which was located on Highway 1056 near the Mt. Pisgah crossroad. Bob Smith stated that he believed that the school steps are still there where the school once stood. (The school site is next to or on Bob Smith's property.) Willie and other students called Mt. Ebal "Dogwood College" because it was a pretty white building surrounded by dogwood trees. In an interview with granddaughter-in-law, Joan Cook, Willie shared a favorite memory from her school days at Mt. Ebal. She recalled, *my classmates and I decided to play hooky one day. Her sister Gladys Burch, cousin Neva Burch, Doris Miller, and Bill Miller got all of the children together and had school out in a field. When the teacher learned what the students had done, she walked through the community that evening telling their parents about the school day. Everybody got a whippin' that night.* Willie recalled how the older students in the school helped the younger students with their school work.

After living in the Burch house on the hill on the Mt. Pisgah road for a couple of years, Earl and Willie moved to the tenant house on the Gene Miller farm. Of course, there was an outdoor toilet behind the house. If toilet paper were available, Mother and Daddy could not afford to buy it or just did not buy it. Like everyone else living during those days, they used the Sears Roebuck catalog for toilet paper. Daddy stated, "When the new catalog arrived, the old one when to the *outhouse*." Daddy hued out a large opening from a log the size of a bath tub creating a place for the family to bathe. In the morning, they filled up the wooden tub with water hand drawn from a well so that the sun could heat the water during the day and have it ready for their baths in the late afternoon.

Mother and Daddy share-cropped with Mallie and Malvern Miller, daughters who obtained the farm from their father Gene Miller, before purchasing the 124 acre farm from Mallie and Malvern Miller on October 17, 1941.

Earl and Willie lived in this Miller house on this farm for over 53 years until his death on January 29, 1994. After Earl passed away, Willie remained in the house for a few years before moving to the Heritage Manor Nursing Home in Franklinton where she died at 86 on January 8, 2002. The Wilkes farm was left to their seven children.

Willie was a very dedicated wife to Earl for 60 years. She worked beside him plowing in the fields, planting and harvesting vegetables from the gardens, milking cows, hauling milk, driving the tractor, doing all house chores and caring for their seven children. She spent her life taking care of the needs of her husband, children, and grandchildren.

At the time of Mother's death, our sister Janice Marie wrote a beautiful tribute to her which reads:

OUR MOTHER
by
Janice Marie Wilkes Branch

A Christian mother who made sure her children grew up knowing the importance of God's Word—always taking the seventh day to rest.

In the beginning, mother worked hard side by side with daddy in the fields of corn and cotton he share-cropped, all the time having and taking care of her precious children.

Mother was a tower of strength in adversity, always putting God first, then family, friends, and community.

Mother was wonderfully talented, whether she was making clothes for her daughters, tending her garden, preparing food, playing the piano and singing her favorite songs

Mother instilled in her children the importance of a Christian life, hardwork, and independence.

Her Motto was, 'Do Unto Others as You Would Have Them Do Unto You.' She left her children with a loving and compassionate nature.

Mother will be dearly missed, but we know it was time for her to dwell in the place, "Where, She'll Never Grow Old."

As one grandson stated, 'Even though Grandma had many grandchildren and great grandchildren, she still made each feel loved.'

When chores were done at home, mother with her special friends, reached the needy, fed the hungry, and helped to take care of their special place of worship. Mother was born and raised in the Mt. Pisgah community, a place from where she never ventured far. It is time for her to rest in a place around the things she so dearly loved and served.

Bobbie Earl, the oldest child of Earl and Willie Wilkes, was assigned to be the executor for our mother upon our father's death on January 29, 1994. Bobbie received from mother a tin file box containing Wilkes records. She took the box to her home for safekeeping. As executor, she provided assistance to mother in maintaining health records, making business transactions, and overseeing the property. Upon Mother's death on January 8, 2002, the Wilkes property was left to their seven children.

What a Treasure

The heirs of the Wilkes property have maintained the home and acreage for eleven years. The heirs came to an agreement on March 13, 2013 to sell the property. In making arrangements to sell, a particular map of the property was needed for a transaction. When Bobbie opened the tin box, she noticed a yellow sheet of paper enclosed in a plastic slip. Recorded below is what she found handwritten by Mother without a date. We do not know when it was written but believe it to have been written prior to our sister Kathy's death on April 2, 1994. We are trying to understand the reason for our discovering this "Letter to My Children" at this time.

A Letter to My Children

Babbie
Dora
Elaine
Faye
Janice
Kathy
Chuck

Would you like to know where I am at, here in my Father's house, in the Mansions prepared for me here - I am where I want to be no longer on the stormy sea, but in God's safe quiet harbor. My sowing time is done and I am reaping my joy is as the joy of harvest. Would you like to know how it is with me? I am made perfect in holiness. Would you like to know what I am doing? I see God, not as through a glass darkly, but face to face. I am engaged in the sweet enjoyment of my precious Saviour. I am singing hallelujahs to him who sits upon the throne, and I am constantly praising him. Would you know what blessed company I keep? It better than the best on earth. I am with many of my old acquaint with whom I worked and prayed, and who have come here before me and since. My problems on earth are now in the hands of God who is a true God. I am comforted knowing that God is in charge, Weep not for me.

Willie Marie Burch Wilkes

116

GETTING TO KNOW EACH OTHER

Gwendora Wilkes and Derry David Magee

The Mt. Hermon community was fairly stable in population due to its being a farming community, primarily dairying. Mt. Hermon consisted of the Mt. Hermon High School, Mt. Hermon Baptist Church, a milk plant, and two or three stores. My sisters and I rode the school bus to MHHS from the Mt. Pisgah community. Our bus ride was approximately 15 miles due to a long bus route that picked up students from surrounding communities.

Derry's Family Moves to Mt. Hermon

In 1949, the Mt. Hermon Baptist Church called as their pastor, Rev. Marvin Magee. Bro. Magee, as he was known as, his wife Mary, son Derry and daughter Mary Jane moved into the parsonage behind the church which was across the road from the MHHS. One can imagine how excited the girls were when Derry Magee, a well-built handsome and intelligent young man, enrolled as a sophomore. The school did not have many new students enrolling and especially a high school student of his caliber.

Naturally, attending a rather small school, our paths crossed daily going to classes, clubs, and basketball practices. Derry, my two sisters and I, along with several other students, took piano classes from Betty Sue Miller during the same year. We all performed in a piano recital together, but I was not aware of his presence at that time.

Having reached the age and grade level to participate in sports at school was very exciting for me. As an eighth grader, I began playing on the Mt. Hermon Junior High girls' softball and basketball teams. As a freshman, I was an active member of 4-H Club, and during the summer, I attended 4-H camp in Denham Springs, La. As a sophomore, I played forward on the Mt. Hermon High School basketball first team, along with my sister Bobbie and first cousin Delores Alford, both played guard.

The high school girls' basketball team practiced in the auditorium (which was the gym at that time) during fifth period of the day. The boys' basketball team practiced during the last period of the day. As our paths crossed during the transition between these daily practices, we began to notice and become aware of each other.

Derry played first team center with my sister Bobbie's husband-to-be, Quinlon McElveen, playing forward. Both girl and boy teams were good, but the boys' team won First Place in the Pine Tournament; defeated the Lumberjacks, the largest and toughest team in the Parish; won the Consolation Trophy in the Kentwood Tournament; and won First Place in the Parish Tournament. During this same year, our sister Dorothy started her successful basketball years by playing on the junior high basketball team.

The school's geometry class, taught by Mrs. Sarah Snell, consisted of four students: Derry Magee, Carol Jean Alford, Glenda Smith and me. I happened to be sitting on the front row with Derry sitting right behind me. I felt someone lightly poking me in the back with a pencil which was the first indication that there might have been some attraction. At some point, Derry asked me to go to church with him during a revival being held at the Mt. Hermon Baptist Church where his father was pastor.

Because the basketball teams practiced during the school day, Derry was able to participate as a basketball player. He was never able to ride the bus to the away games with the other basketball players because of his commitment to his dairy farm which was his plan for making money to attend veterinary school. His dad drove him to the games after he had completed milking.

While Derry was in high school and operating his dairy, he rode a horse from the parsonage to his farm every morning to milk cows by hand. He rode back home on horseback to bathe, eat and get ready for school. He followed the same routine in the afternoon riding the horse to the farm and back home.

The principal's son had been harassing Derry at school. Because Derry was never allowed to fight, he went to his dad and told him what was going on. His dad advised him to talk to the principal. Derry talked to the principal, and the issue was resolved.

On the bus ride to play a basketball game at Spring Creek High School one evening, the principal's son decided to sit by me on the bus. He reached over to hold my hand, but I resisted. Just before we departed the bus, this ball player reached over and smacked me on the cheek. This was quite a surprise!

Leadership has always been a part of my and Derry's motivation. As a freshman, I served as class president. During the year 1951, I served as Vice-President of the Future Homemakers of America club. That same year, Derry served as Reporter of the Future Farmers of America club and was voted "Most Likely to Succeed." In 1952, he was valedictorian of his senior class with a 4.0 GPA.

One evening as Derry was driving me home from a date, he expressed to me that I was the one he would marry and spend the rest of his life with. His dream for us was to have a white house on a hill with a white board fence.

When we moved to Kentwood where he practiced veterinary medicine for 32 years, we bought a house on a small hill on the edge of town from Dr. Robert Blades at 515 Third Street which was on Highway 51 N. Upon acquiring a horse, it called for the building of a white board fence on the property. Derry fulfilled his promise. He had gotten me that white house on a hill with a white board fence.

Other dates included dating in our living room or going to the "picture show" in Franklinton where we enjoyed the western shows with Roy Rogers and Gene Autry. One evening Derry came to my house and learned that my family had planned to go to the movie in town. Derry did not have any money for our admission to the movie theatre, so he borrowed $.25 from my Daddy.

Daddy had rented a field from Mr. Fleet Miller just behind the Mt. Hermon School where he planted corn. Because I was Daddy's tractor driver, and he needed help with the plowing, I did not attend school on that day. At lunch time, Daddy and I walked over to the school cafeteria to eat lunch because there was not an eating place at Mt. Hermon. Derry tells the story that when he saw me walk into the cafeteria that day, he thought that I was the most beautiful girl he had ever seen. This started the beginning of a two-year courtship before we were married in 1952.

Derry also planted corn for cow feed. During the spring of 1951, he became ill and couldn't "lay by" his corn. I asked Daddy if I could take our tractor to Derry's farm and plow his corn. Daddy gave me permission and support as I drove the tractor several miles to Derry's farm. Derry and I were always together as our schedules and opportunities would allow.

Derry graduated Mt. Hermon High School in May, 1952, as Valedictorian and began his freshman year in Pre-veterinary Medicine at Louisiana State University during that summer. I was so thrilled to see him when he came to visit me after completing the summer session. He returned home to help with the farm responsibilities and to prepare for the fall semester at LSU. We were married on October 11, 1952 which allowed us to begin our life's journey together as he pursued his dream of becoming a veterinarian.

Derry and I, with the help of Uncle Dorman and Aunt Margaret Burch, located an apartment on West Roosevelt St., just outside the LSU gate on Nicholson Drive in Baton Rouge, La. We were blessed to have a three-room apartment with a living room, bedroom and kitchen for $50.00 (utilities included) a month and sharing a bath with a couple in the two-front apartment for the first year at LSU.

When Derry and I moved to our first apartment on West Roosevelt, Grandma Bridges caught the Greyhound bus to Baton Rouge from Ponchatoula to help us get settled in our first apartment. We used the Baton Rouge city bus to ride to downtown Baton Rouge to shop for needed items. Grandma walked a few blocks from our house to the grocery store to get food items to cook. This is when I was first introduced to rutabagas, cabbage, red beans, lima beans, and black-eyed peas.

We did not grow these food items on our farm, but we did grow turnips, mustard, fresh peas, butterbeans, string beans, potatoes, etc. People who lived in the city ate foods purchased in the grocery stores while those of us who were raised on the farm, ate fresh vegetables grown in our gardens.

Grandma Bridges' was an excellent cook. Her cooking was influenced by the many years that she lived in New Orleans. She knew how much Derry loved red beans; therefore, she always made sure he had a pot of red beans to eat while she was visiting. Red beans have become one of our favorite foods seasoned with a good hambone.

At the end of Derry's first year in Pre-vet at LSU, we returned to Mt. Hermon for the summer for Derry to work on his dairy farm. We rented an apartment in the front of the Fleet and Bessie Miller historic home. The apartment included a very spacious bedroom, a kitchen, and bath.

One night I remained in the apartment with our newly born daughter Juanita, while Derry walked over to the MHS softball field to play ball. I was lying in bed with the lights out when all of a sudden a bright glow appeared at the foot of my bed. I received Jesus Christ as my Saviour at that moment, and upon Derry's return from the ball game, I asked him if he knew Jesus as his Saviour. He stated that he did, and his life exemplifies this to have been true.

I had joined the church in my early youth during a revival—I suppose I was just following the other young people who went down to join the church and was baptized in the swimming hole at Silver Creek. When I was in my late 30's, I became convicted that I had not followed Biblical teachings in that baptism follows Salvation. At First Baptist Church in Kentwood, I went forward during an invitation to ask for baptism which I received later.

When we returned to LSU in the fall for Derry's sophomore year, the two-room apartment in the front of this same house on

West Roosevelt was available for $40.00 a month which we were happy to have.

At the end of Derry's sophomore year in Pre-vet at LSU, we returned to the family farm where we lived in the spacious farm house while getting ready to move to Texas A&M for him to begin his studies as a veterinary student in the Veterinary School in the fall of 1954. We lived in College Station four years until Derry graduated Veterinary Medicine in 1958.

SPORTS
A Wilkes Family Tradition

GROWING UP IN A COMMUNITY with a small school, basketball, baseball, and softball were the three main sports played. My parents, Earl and Willie Wilkes, and their seven children played softball and basketball in school. Baseball was a male sport. Our parents were excellent basketball players when they played on the Mt. Hermon High School basketball teams. Several years after high school, Mother played on a softball team with older ladies who had played in high school. Our parents were very supportive in helping to keep the basketball family tradition alive with all of their seven children playing and excelling in basketball at MHHS.

Basketball Became the Major Sport

During the 1951-52 school year, my sister Bobbie and I played on the Girls Basketball first team. Bobbie Earl played guard, and I played forward. Mother and Daddy were very excited when we made the team and were faithful to attend our games.

One night, we were playing Enon High School that had a forward player who ran very fast down the court to the goal. She ran Bobbie over several times causing her to hit the floor. Daddy pulled Bobbie to the side and told her, *if you allow that girl to run you over again, you will get a spanking when you get home.* The player did not run Bobbie over again. Bobbie stopped her in her tracks, putting an end to her drives to the goal.

Our sister Dorothy Elaine played on the Mt. Hermon Junior High Basketball team during this year. She was an excellent shooter from the outer court and foul line, scoring high points throughout her high school years. She married Cleatus Cook, her teacher and the boys' basketball coach, and continued playing on the team until she graduated high school. She was coached by Mrs. Mary Dickey, one of the best women coaches in the area.

Mt. Hermon Girls Win State in 1962

In 1962, our sisters, Janice Marie and Faye Ellen played on the Mt. Hermon Girls State Class B Basketball Championship team. In this championship game, the team played one of the most perfect and spectacular games that we have ever seen played. The players moved the ball on the ball court like a well-oiled machine under the coaching of Mary Dickey. Mrs. Dickey was an excellent coach who taught her team the proper basketball skills and had them practice until they had mastered the skills. She was a very tough and competitive coach who got the best effort from her ball players.

At basketball practice one afternoon, Faye became so angry at Mrs. Dickey for her toughness and high expectations that she turned in her ball suit—meaning that she had quit. When she arrived home from school, she told Daddy what she had done. He marched her right back to the school to apologize to Mrs. Dickey and to retrieve her suit. She remained on the team and became such an outstanding ball player that she was named a State Guard in 1962. Faye did not allow the mumps to keep her from playing in one of the state playoff games.

The night that they won the State Championship game, Mr. Schilling, a long time basketball fan and supporter of Mt. Hermon High basketball teams, was present. In all of the excitement from the win, he came up to Faye and Daddy and congratulated Faye on a well-played game. Faye said, "Thank you." Daddy said to her "What?" Knowing what she knew she should have said, she quickly said to Mr. Schilling, "Thank you, sir." Mother and Daddy taught us to always respect our elders by saying, "yes mam and no mam" and "yes sir and no sir." It is very sad that some families do not teach their children the proper respect for adults. It is also disappointing that children who are taught to say these respectful words are punished for saying them to certain people and in some classrooms.

Our parents taught us to *hang tough when the going got rough*. We were never allowed to quit when things did not go our way. Allowing Faye to quit could have cost the team the State Championship and denied her the honor of being named an All State Guard.

Mt. Hermon Girls Win State in 1964

In 1964, our sister Janice Marie played forward on the Mt. Hermon High Class B State Championship team setting a scoring record against Block High School in the 1964 semifinals. According to the LHSAA Basketball publication, Janice still holds the Class B individual scoring record by scoring 49 points—Most Points One Game and holds the record for the Most Point Scored in Two Games in 1964. After winning the Championship game, the coach from Walker High School came over and told us that Janice deserved to take the Championship trophy home with her, and we agreed.

Our youngest sister Kathy had four successful years playing guard under Coach Mary Dickey. Our brother, Chuck Wilkes who is 6'4" tall, played on the boys basketball team that experienced some great wins during his high school years under his brother-in-law Coach Cleatus Cook.

Daddy loved the game of basketball and was very committed to helping his children and grandchildren become the very best that they could be on the ball court. He went to the MHHS gym in the afternoons after school and on weekends to throw the ball back to Janice while she practiced her shooting. Janice used every opportunity to practice shooting baskets at school and at home on a dirt court in our yard to become the very best.

Pamela Cook and Tamela Cook, daughters of Coach Cook and Dorothy Elaine, played in the 1974 Class C Basketball State Championship game for Mt. Hermon. Bobbie's youngest daughter, Kim McElveen, also played on this team.

Pamela (Pam) was name MVP in the First Women's All Star Basketball game in Louisiana; received the First Female Basketball Scholarship to LSU; named an All-American player for two years in a row while playing at Southeastern Louisiana University; was an outstanding player when SLU won the National Women's Basketball Championship in Pomona, CA; and played in the A.I.A.W.'s First All-American Women's Basketball game in Washington, D.C. In 1998, Pam was inducted into SLU's Athletic Hall of Fame, and in 2005, she was inducted into the LHSAA Hall of Fame.

Pam and Tam had exceptional natural athletic abilities but learned many basketball skills and techniques from Coach Dickey, their father Coach Cook, and grandfather "PawPaw" Earl Wilkes. After the girls basketball team qualified to compete for the state championship games, Mrs. Dickey or Coach Puckett, always enlisted Coach Cook to help prepare the girls for the state playoff games. Coach Cook was always present on the coaching bench with the girls coaches during the playoff games. "PawPaw" Earl was always on a bench nearby quietly coaching and cheering the players on during these games. "PawPaw" went to the MHHS gym after school and on weekends standing under the goal throwing the ball back to Pam for her to practice shooting just as he had done for his daughter Janice Wilkes ten years earlier.

Pam Cook and Craig Forrest's two children, Trent and Traci Forrest, were outstanding basketball players at Sumner High School, Spring Creek, La. Trent earned numerous MVP awards during high school (1994-1997), scoring over 1000 points. In the summer of 1997, he played in the High School All-Star game which made Trent the third generation member of his family to play in this HS All-Star game in 1997. His grandfather Cleatus Cook coached in a High School All-Star game; and his mother

Pamela Cook played in a High School All-Star game. Trent played basketball at Southwest Junior College and later attended and graduated Millsaps College in Jackson, Mississippi. He played basketball at Millsaps during the time that they became Conference Champions in 2001.

Traci Forrest played for Sumner High School earning numerous MVP awards (1997-2000). She played for Southwest Junior College where she was named Junior College ALL-STAR and played in the Junior College All Star game in Philadelphia, MS.

Among other grandchildren who followed the Wilkes basketball tradition at MHHS, were two of Bobbie's children: Cheryl and Craig McElveen who participated in basketball. Due to asthma, Bobbie's oldest daughter Beverly McElveen was unable to play sports, but she attended the games, keeping the statistics for the girls and boys teams.

Beverly has collected a treasure of MHHS basketball memorabilia that is on display in the hallway outside the school gym. In addition to Dorothy Cook's two daughters playing for Mt. Hermon, her two sons Brad and Randy Cook had some very successful high school years playing for their father Coach Cook on the school's boys basketball team. The athletic tradition of the Wilkes family playing basketball at MHHS continued as Bobbie's granddaughters and Beverly's daughters, Melissa Walker (1996-2000) and Shea Taylor (2006-2011) played for the Yellow Jackets.

Bobbie's grandson "Mac" McElveen, son of Craig McElveen, is a very gifted basketball player who reminds Derry and me of his grandfather Quinlon McElveen on the ball court. He plays forward for the Bowling Green Buchaneers and has received several basketball awards and will continue excelling as he matures physically and athletically.

Families Value Sports and Education

After Derry graduated Texas A&M Veterinary School in 1958, we moved back to Louisiana, first to Amite and then to Kentwood in Tangipahoa Parish where he began practicing. Our daughter Nita attended kindergarten in Amite, La. and began first grade at Kentwood Elementary School.

While attending Kentwood High School, Nita played basketball as a left-handed forward on the Junior and Senior girls basketball teams. Her coach was very easy-going and never applied any pressure on the girls. Nita loved to play the game of basketball and during high school competition she had developed some skills that prepared her to join the girls basketball team at Mississippi College, Clinton, Mississippi, in 1969 as a freshmen. She remained on the team until the running caused blisters on her feet hindering her ability to run. At that time, she decided to focus on her academics and other college activities. She used her athletic talents in performing as a member of the Choctaw dance group during halftime at the Mississippi College Choctaw Indians football games. She was a runner-up in the Miss Mississippi College Pageant.

Steve, her husband-to-be, played junior and high school football at Gulfport East High and High School football at Biloxi High School. Upon graduating high school, he received a four-year football scholarship to play defensive end for the Choctaws at Mississippi College. Steve and Nita met in the cafeteria at MC which ultimately brought them together as a couple.

After dating two years, Nita and Steve married in 1972. They continued their education and both graduated from MC in 1974. Steve received a degree in Business Administration and Nita received a degree in Biology. Steve coached football as a graduate assistant while completing his MBA at Mississippi College. Nita worked at the Veterans Administration in research. After receiving his MBA, Steve joined the Hinds Junior Community College as a teacher and as an assistant coach in Raymond, Mississippi. After leaving Hinds following five football seasons, he moved to Miami, FL and entered teaching and coaching at Palmetto High School. He has continued to coach football and teach in various public and private schools in the Miami, Florida area. He is presently teaching and coaching defense at Christopher Columbus Catholic High School in Miami.

Our granddaughter, Jennifer Jean Johnson, Nita and Steve's oldest child, played basketball as a ninth grader at Palmetto Middle School in Miami. She was an athletic trainer during her four years at Palmetto High School where her Daddy was defensive coach for several years. As a college student, she continued working as a trainer for Mississippi Southern University and Pearl River Junior College in Mississippi. She had to give up her dream of becoming an athletic trainer or pursuing any other scientific career because she is highly allergic to formaldehyde which she encountered in all of her science classes. She continued her education at the Florida International University (FIU) in Miami, FL, receiving a degree in Business Management.

Jennifer spent her entire life attending all of the sports that her brothers and father were and still involved in. She has become one of the most knowledgeable females about the football teams, players, and the game. She plays Fantasy Football on-line and usually beats all of the males who are participating.

This past year, a group of friends decided that Jennifer needed to join their kickball team. They quickly learned that the first thing that they had to do was teach her how run before working on other kickball skills. She works very hard at everything that she does, but she is not an athlete. She is a beautiful young lady who has never liked to sweat.

Our oldest grandson, William Derry "Bill" Johnson, is one of the most gifted athletes we have ever known. When he was four or five years old, he dove from the high diving board at the Kentwood Aquatic Club without hesitating. He was an excellent swimmer, runner, football player, and baseball player. He played nine years (ages 6-14) in the Khoury Baseball League with Steve his daddy as his coach for many years. Steve spent many afternoons in their backyard throwing and pitching baseballs to him. Steve also spent hours throwing the football to Bill. Bill played football in grades 6-11, but baseball was his first love.

During his high school years, he played on the Palmetto High School baseball team as center fielder. He attended colleges on a baseball scholarship, graduating Trevecca Nazarene University in Nashville, TN in accounting. Bill had the skills, talent, and speed to be a professional baseball player, but the opportunity never arose. He has been referred to as having been the fastest white boy in Miami, FL.

Ross Melvin Johnson, our youngest grandchild, is an excellent student and an outstanding baseball player and football player. He played baseball during his 6-10 grades and played football from 9-12 grades. He played defensive end at Westminster Christian School for two years. He played tight end for the Christopher Columbus Catholic High School football team in Miami during his last two years in high school. He received a four year football scholarship to play tight end at Ave Maria University, Ave Maria, FL during the 2011-2012 school year. He is 6'5" and weighs approximately 200 pounds. He is presently playing tight end and defensive end at Ave Maria University and plans to major in pharmacy.

The Wilkes great-grandchildren who did not actually play a sport participated as cheerleaders, drill team members, band members, and statisticians. Most of the female grandchildren and great-grandchildren of Earl and Willie Wilkes played some kind of sport, became good students, and some were named beauty queens in their schools and communities. Even though all the Wilkes descendants have loved and participated in sports, they have found pursuing an education beyond high school has contributed to their becoming very successful in their careers.

"Old Coaches Never Die"

Coach Cleatus Cook started his basketball journey on a dirt court outside the school gym at White Oak, Miss. A boyhood handicap forced him to play basketball harder to compete against boys with healthy legs. He had polio as a kid and wore leg braces until he was 14. He then threw the braces away and "got after it." He still walked with a limp, but it never bothered him too much in high school. Cleatus learned basketball "from the ground up" literally at White Oak. The Junior High basketball players couldn't play in the gym until they were in high school. In Junior High, they gathered some poles and boards and made a basketball court on the school ground and played on dirt. He was pretty scrappy all through high school and believed that his players at Mt. Hermon High School played that way for him.

Coach Cook might have been able to play some Junior College basketball at Jones County Junior College in Ellisville, Miss., if he could have gone home on the weekends. After the college coach told him that making the team meant that there would not be any trips home until Christmas, he figured that was taking too much from a youngster who hadn't been outside Smith County many times during his life. After graduating college at Southern Mississippi at Hattiesburg, Miss., he coached a year in Mississippi and then "latched" onto the job at Mt. Hermon High School teaching and coaching in 1953.

After achieving great success coaching the boys basketball teams for 27 years at MHHS, he retired and continued his love of coaching at several private schools. His coaching experience and expertise taught these private school basketball players how to play and achieve success in competitions. When he was no longer able to coach, he was on the sidelines cheering for his grandchildren.

My Love of Teaching

DERRY AND I HAVE ONE CHILD, a daughter, Juanita Elaine Magee, whom we call Nita. She skipped her senior year at Kentwood High School in Kentwood, LA. At the end of her high school junior year, she qualified to enter Mississippi College early without receiving a high school diploma. Mississippi College is a Baptist college, located in Clinton, Mississippi approximately 100 miles from Kentwood where Nita grew up. Having Nita this close to home allowed Derry and me to participate in some of her campus activities. Derry always stated, "Mississippi College was like a buffer zone, allowing Nita to be away from home living on a small Baptist college campus with established Christian values like her own." When my friends heard that I had made a trip to Mississippi College, they asked, "What did Nita need, a pencil?" Nita received a degree in Biology and later received her Bachelor of Science in Nursing Degree in Miami, FL.

While attending Mississippi College, she met her husband, Steven Winslow Johnson, who played defensive end on the MC football team. He was a business major who later received an MBA at MC while he served as a graduate assistant working in the MC football program. He teaches and coaches football at Christopher Columbus Catholic High School in Miami, FL.

Nita and Steven married during the summer of 1972 before they began their junior years of college. They both graduated in May of 1974 and remained a few years in the Jackson and Raymond, Mississippi where they both worked. They were very busy working and building their lives together. Nita no longer needed a "pencil" which meant that I could be working toward a profession.

After the Kentwood schools became integrated in 1969, most of the white students left Kentwood High School and joined private schools that sprung up all around. This caused a great need for substitute teachers at KHS. I applied and was accepted without a college degree. I enjoyed teaching and working with the high school students so much that I became motivated to become a teacher. Since, Nita was married and living away, and Derry was very busy in his veterinary practice, this was the perfect time for me to begin my education journey. In 1974, I enrolled at Southeastern Louisiana University in Hammond, La. The drive to SLU was approximately 35 miles from my home in Kentwood. I traveled to and from SLU three to five days a week depending on my class schedule.

In 1978, I received my first degree in Business Education. I taught at SLU as a graduate assistant while receiving a Master's in Business Education. Having received a minor in English in 1980, KHS hired me to teach English (grades 9-12) and a bookkeeping class. I continued attending classes at SLU at night, receiving a Specialist in Education degree in 1984.

While teaching at KHS, I became very intrigued with why some students could not read. When an opening came in the Special Education department, I asked my principal if I could transfer from English to the Special Education classes. He very reluctantly agreed and stated that the school's ACT scores would go down without my teaching senior English. This was a win-win situation for the school, me, and a Junior High English teacher who had wanted to move to the high school English classroom. She has done a super job of keeping the standards set for the students who planned to attend college.

While teaching English and bookkeeping, I sponsored the BETA Club and the school newspaper. The KHS football team was state champions several years in a row with articles written about them in the *Baton Rouge Morning Advocate*. I asked an outstanding star football player from my English classroom to write an article for our newspaper about the Kentwood-Greensburg game which was a big rival game. This student had never learned to read; therefore, he enlisted his cousin to write the account of the game as he dictated it. She printed by hand the copy for him to print in his handwriting. The sentences were very short and contained his name several times in the article which was o.k. I typed the article and printed it for him to distribute to the students.

This "Language Experience Approach to Reading" was how this student began to read. As he was learning to read, he went to the school library every day to read the newspaper articles written about his school's football team. The student shared this success story with me when Derry and I drove to Southwest Junior College to watch him play football. While visiting with him after the game, he proudly shared with us that he had read the *Beowulf* poem for his first time in his college English class. His success was my reward for teaching at KHS for ten years before moving to Texas.

Teaching the special education students at KHS was very enjoyable and rewarding. When I took over the high school special education self-contained class, they had been playing cards with the teacher and assistant during the school day. I took down all curtains that covered the windows, and "school began." The students became committed to learning and respected me greatly. I took them on field trips that related to the curriculum lessons.

While teaching these students, I continued my studies in special education at SLU. I used the methods and strategies that I learned at SLU while receiving my Master's in Special Education and Gifted/Talented Education, but I used my God given talents in teaching and reaching these students. After graduating KHS, most of these students attended some institution of higher learning and trade schools. One student who was a track star received a track scholarship to a small college. When I left the school to join my husband in Texas, the students and parents with tears asked, "Who is going to look after our children"? These ten years at KHS were the most enjoyable and rewarding years of my teaching career.

As soon as I completed the 1989-90 school year, I moved to College Station, TX to be with my husband who had left his Kentwood veterinary practice in March, 1990 to join the Large Animal Medicine and Surgery Department in the College of Veterinary Medicine at Texas A&M University. We moved into a one bedroom condo for three months until we could find a house.

We purchased a new three bedroom house at 1004 Laredo Court in College Station that had just been completed. We did not move any furniture and appliances from our large home in Kentwood, LA, because we wanted our Kentwood house ready for us and our family whenever we went back to visit. For our Texas house, we purchased mattresses and box springs, a couch and chairs, a dinette set, a washer and dryer which was all that we needed in the smaller house. We lived there 16 years in the house with 1200 square feet of floor space. Juanwood, our home in Kentwood, La., contained approximately 5,000 square feet setting on 20 acres of wooded land. It was a special refuge for us, our family and friends. We traveled back to Juanwood every three or four months to maintain the house and the yard. We sold Juanwood in 2006 after we decided that we would retire in College Station to be near the medical facilities.

In 1990, when I interviewed with the College Station Independent School District, I told them that I would be willing to teach wherever they wanted to assign me. I could have taught English and business classes in all grade levels at the high school. I also was certified to teach special education and gifted education at all grade levels, K-12. I was assigned to teach the Language Arts Resource classes at the fifth and sixth grade levels which were housed at Oakwood Middle School with Gerald Wynn serving as principal. Later the district adopted the Renzulli Enrichment Triad Model to serve the gifted and talented students. This program called for an Enrichment Coordinator on each campus to meet the needs of all students.

I was asked to serve as Enrichment Coordinator at Oakwood Middle School and served in this role for three years. I dearly enjoyed seeing students identify their talents and gifts through this Renzulli Triad Model. Activities were provided for students to expand and enrich their knowledge and understanding of their interests. For instance, if students were interested in geology, I arranged for TAMU students to bring samples of rocks for students to see and identify various kinds of rocks. If students were interested in horses, I had an Equine professor come to teach them about horses and their special capabilities. Upon the completion of a Type III project chosen by the student according

135

to his/her interest, the student presented the investigation to an audience.

In 1995, Ms. Sue Ashburn, an outstanding woman and school principal at Southwood Valley Elementary School campus, hired me to serve as Academic Coordinator/Assistant Principal. I assisted with curriculum, staff development, textbook inventory, discipline, evaluation of teachers and staff, school newsletter, workshops, and other responsibilities.

One of my most enjoyable experiences as AC was inviting 4-5 students each day during each 30 minute lunch period. The students brought their lunches to my office where I read the "Starfish" poem which expresses how special each starfish is. During this time of sitting and eating at the round table allowed the students time for conversation and the freedom to talk about anything. Several student conflicts were resolved around this table.

By the end of each school year, I had the privilege of visiting with approximately 250 students. Students who had moved on to other campuses came back to me later and thanked me for that special time in my office. Parents also expressed to me how special those lunch times were for their children. Spending quality time with these students was an additional reward as an administrator!

I served as Academic Coordinator for approximately 12 years before retiring in 2007, the same year my husband, Dr. Derry Magee, retired from the Large Animal and Surgery Department of the College of Veterinary Medicine at Texas A&M University.

Derry and I are enjoying retirement after my 27 years of service in education and his 32 years as a practicing veterinarian in private practice followed by his practicing and teaching 17 years at Texas A&M for a total of 49 years in veterinary medicine. We thoroughly enjoy spending time together. We really treasure our mornings since we do not have to get up at a certain time to rush off to work. We leisurely drink our cups of coffee each morning. We are careful not to schedule any doctor appointments before 10:00 a.m.

Genealogy Records

A. Derry's Great-Grandparents and Grandparents

MAGEE ANCESTORS

Genealogists and historians have referenced accounts of the Magee lines being traced back to Jeremiah 43:5-7, an early King of Scotland and an early King of Ireland, ca 400 AD. (Scota who was a daughter of King Zedekiah became Queen of Scotland.)

Alpin, King of Scotland, Ascended the Scottish throne in 787 A.D. and died in 834 A.D.

Prince Gregor, Third son of Alpin had two sons

Constantine married Malvina, daughter of Donald VI, king of Scotland.

Gregor, elder son of Constantine and Malvina, married Dorbiggdda. He died about 961 in a battle with the Danes.

John, oldest son of Gregor married Alpine, daughter of Angus - died about 1004.

Gregor, Laird of Glenuchy, fought under Duncan 1 against the Normans and Danes. He married a daughter of Campell of Lochnow.
Sir John, Gregor's son, married the daughter of Henry, Prince of Scotland, and died in 1238.

Malcolm, Lord of McGregor, son of Sir John, married Mary daughter of Malise McAlpin. Malcon died in 1374. He had two sons.

Gregor, Lord MacGregor (from whom is descended our line of Magees), married Iris MacAlpin daughter of Malcom MacAlpin. He died in 1461.

John MacGregor, son of Gregor, He married first a MacLaughlin, second a Macintosh and third Helen Campbell.

Gregor MacGregor, second son of John and MacLaughlin married Finvola (Flora) MacArthur ofStrachur.
Duncan MacGregor, son of Gregor, married Mary, daughter of Lord Ardkinlass.

Gregor McGregor, son of Duncan, married Isabella Cameron, daughter of The Chieftain of Sicrnhead. Second marriage to a Christian MacFarland.

Patrick MacGregor, married Marlan MacLeod. He is also recorded as marrying Lady Marian McDonald of Auchtrichatan. It is recorded that he was quite an outlaw in the highlands in 1636. Duncan MacGregor, eldest son of Gregor and MacFarline, was born Lochabar. (About 1844—Perthshire)

James MacGregor was born about 1645, died 1724. He married Ann Bastrop in 1676. She was born in 1656 in County Kent, England. James died after July 27, 1727. James fought in his father's clan for the cause of King Charles 1. As punishment for fighting with the losing side in this war, members of the MacGregor clan were ordered to change their names. James changed his name to *Thomas Mackgeehee.* He immigrated to Virginia, USA, in about 1650

William MACGEEHEE was the son of Thomas and Ann. He was born in New Kent City, Virginia in 1677. He died in 1747 in Caroline County, VA.

William, Jr. was born in 1722 and married Elizabeth McCulloch.

JOHN MACGEEHEE was born in 1736/42. He was the son of William, Jr. MACGEEHEE. He married Ann Moore in 1754 at the age of 18.

PHILLIP MAGEE was born in 1770 to John and Ann MACGEEHEE in Duplin County, North Carolina. He married Mary Butler (1773-1860) in North Carolina. They had six children. Phillip died in 1826.

SOLOMAN MAGEE was born on Jan. 29, 1795 and died August 18, 1826. He married Elizabeth Weathersby.

WILLIS SIMS MAGEE was born on July 2, 1818 and died on August 14, 1883. (Disease of the heart) He married Mary Norwood.

ROBERT SOLOMAN MAGEE was born on March 2, 1845 and died on Dec. 3, 1888. He married Eugenia Elizabeth Mangum. Eugenia was born on Oct. 12, 1846 in MS and died on Mar. 3, 1927 in MS. She was buried in Magee Cemetery of Covington County, MS.

DERRY DAVID MAGEE was born on May 20, 1866 and died on Oct. 27, 1929. (Brights Disease) He married Zora Easterling on August 23, 1903. Zora was born in 1884 and died in 1921 of stomach cancer. They had three children.

MARVIN MANGUM MAGEE was born on July 18, 1908 in Collins, MS. He died on January 6, 1971 in Amite County, MS of a heart attack. He married Mary Alline Bridges on October 25, 1931 in Collins, MS. Mary was born on August 22, 1914 in Liberty, MS and died on Sept. 18, 1990. They are both buried in the Line Creek Baptist Church Cemetery in La.

DERRY DAVID MAGEE was born in New Orleans on July 5, 1934 to Marvin Mangum Magee and Mary Alline Bridges Magee. He married Gwendora Wilkes on October 11, 1952. Gwendora was born on Sept. 1, 1936 to Earl Samuel Wilkes and Willie Burch Wilkes. They had one daughter: Juanita Elaine Magee.

JUANITA ELAINE MAGEE was born on May 3, 1953 to Derry and Gwendora Magee. Juanita married Steven Winslow Johnson on August 11, 1972 in Kentwood, La. Steven was born on Sept. 2, 1952. They have three children:

Jennifer Jean Johnson(March 16, 1978)

William Derry "Bill" Johnson(Feb. 10, 1980) m. Kellye Danielle Staudt - b.May 21, 1982 Their children:

Mia Mckenzie Johnson (Jan. 17, 2008)
William Chase Johnson (Dec. 20, 2010)

Ross Melvin Johnson (Oct. 29, 1991)

EASTERLING ANCESTORS

The Easterling surname of the oldest known and can be traced back to Germanic tribes who lived in the Baltic Sea area about 1,000 AD or earlier.

Possible Line of Descent

HENRY EASTERLING of Calvert County, Maryland

HENRY EASTERLING Jr. of Calvert County, Maryland

The Rev. HENRY EASTERLING of North and South Carolina was born May 24, 1733 and died March 26, 1800. He married Elizabeth (Ellen, or Elizabeth Ellen) Bennett in or near Dobbs or Duplin County, Georgia in about 1753-1754.

HENRY EASTERLING was the tenth child born to the Rev. Henry Easterling and Elizabeth Bennett around 1776. He married Margaret Laird (Lard) with whom he had nine children.

JOHN EASTERLING was born in 1801 to Henry Easterling and Margaret Laird. He died about 1845. He married Elizabeth Grantham in about 1831, and they had at least seven children.

HENRY W. EASTERLING was born about 1833 to John Easterling and Elizabeth Grantham. Date of death unknown. He married Mary McDonald in about 1855, and they had least six children.

JOHN CALVIN EASTERLING born on November 4, 1856 to Henry W. Easterling and Mary McDonald. John died April 30, 1931. He married Susan Dees who was born in 1858 and died in 1943. John and Susan had eleven children.

ZORA EASTERLING was born July 19, 1884 and died May 21, 1921. She married DERRY DAVID MAGEE who was born on May 20, 1866 and died October 27, 1929. He married Zora on August 23, 1903. They had three children.

MARVIN MANGUM MAGEE was born July 18, 1908 and died January 6, 1971. He married Mary Alline Bridges on Oct. 25, 1931. Mary was born August 22, 1914 and died on Sept. 8, 1990. They had three children.

DERRY DAVID MAGEE was born on July 5, 1934 in New Orleans, La. He married Gwendora Wilkes on October 11, 1952. Gwendora was born on Sept. 1, 1936 to Earl and Willie Wilkes. Derry and Gwendora had one child: Juanita Elaine Magee.

JUANITA ELAINE MAGEE was born on May 3, 1953 in Tylertown, Miss. to Derry and Gwendora Magee. On August 11, 1972, she married Steven Winslow Johnson who was born on Sept. 2, 1952. Their children:

Jennifer Jean Johnson (March 16, 1978)

William Derry "Bill" Johnson(Feb. 10, 1980) m. Kellye Danielle Staudt (May 21, 1982). Their children:
Mia Mckenzie Johnson (Jan. 17, 2008)
William Chase Johnson (Dec. 20, 2010)

Ross Melvin Johnson

BANKSTON ANCESTORS

JOHN BANKSTON
(1754-1823)

HENRIETTA COATES
(1778-1838)

PETER BANKSTON
(Nov. 9, 1816-Feb. 4, 1880)

TABITHA ROBERTSON
(Nov. 29, 1794-Dec. 25, 1871)

ENOCH COURTNEY
(May 8, 1799-1853+)

MARY ANN HUMBLE
(Nov. 30, 1805-1853+)

BOLEYN ROBERTSON BANKSTON
(Nov. 9, 1816-Feb. 4, 1880)

ELIZA JANE COURTNEY
(Mar. 7, 1825-Feb. 17, 1863)

THOMAS JEFFERSON BANKSTON
(Dec. 20, 1856-Sept. 7, 1942)

MARY E. VERNON
(Feb. 2, 1858-April 17, 1898)

JUANITA RIVERS BANKSTON
(July 15, 1885-Oct. 5, 1965)

CANNON W. BRIDGES
(March 22, 1852-1923)

MARY ALLINE BRIDGES
(Aug. 22, 1914-Sept. 8, 1990)

MARVIN M. MAGEE
(July 18, 1908-Jan. 6, 1971)

DERRY DAVID MAGEE
(July 5, 1934)

GWENDORA WILKES
(Sept. 1, 1936)

JUANITA ELAINE MAGEE
(May 3, 1953)

STEVEN W. JOHNSON
(Sept. 2, 1952)

Their children:
JENNIFER JEAN JOHNSON –b. Mar. 16, 1978

WILLIAM DERRY "BILL" JOHNSON – b. Feb. 10, 1980
married Kellye Danielle Staudt –b. May 21, 1982
    Their children:
        Mia McKenzie Johnson - b. Jan. 17, 2008
        William Chase Johnson –b. Dec. 20, 2010

ROSS MELVIN JOHNSON – b. Oct. 29, 1991

BRIDGES ANCESTORS

Genealogy traced back to the 30th Generation in Lancashire, England
Prepared by Dr. Charles Bridges, grandson of Cannon Bridges

30th	Marmuduke TULKETH Saxon lord of Tulketh, Lancashire, England
29th	Arnold TRAVERS - died c1125
28th	John TRAVERS-died March 19, 1188 in Tulketh Castle
27th	Lawrence TRAVERS – died 1238 in Lancashire, England
26th	Lawrence Fitz TRAVERS – died 1287 in Tulketh Castle
25th	Thomas TRAVERS – b. 1251 d. c1334
24th	Lawrence TRAVERS – d. 1346
23rd	Thomas TRAVERS - d. 1364+ in Tulketh Castle
22nd	John TRAVERS – d. Oct. 29, 1361
21st	Roger TRAVERS – b. 1354
20th	Thomas TRAVERS – born in Tulketh Castle
19th	Laurence TRAVERS – d. 1452+ in Tulketh Castle
18th	Robert TRAVERS – born in Tulketh Castle and d. 1479 in France
17th	Captain Royal Army Richard TRAVERS - d. in North Isle of Minister, Cantebury
16th	William TRAVERS – d. July 28, 1524 in Scotland
15th	William, Jr. TRAVIS - d. July 24, 1558 and buried in Furness Abbey
14th	Richard TRAVIS – b. 1541 in Nateby Hall and Tulketh and d. April 10, 1576
13th	William TRAVIS - b. July, 1563 in Nateby Hall, Lancashire, England - d. Feb. 21, 1627
12th	William TRAVIS – b. c1597 in Nateby Hall d. Sept. 22, 1664, London, England
11th	William III TRAVIS – b. 1624, Brandon Cork, Ireland – d. 1685 in N.C. referred to as the immigrant to America
10th	Daniel TRAVIS – b. 1669 in Rhode Island or Virginia – d. 1696

9th	Doctor Dr. Edward TRAVIS – b. North Carolina – d. Dec. 30, 1739
8th	Lt. Col. (Militia) John Sr. (Son of Dr. Edward T.) TRAVIS – b. in 1715 in N.C. – d. 1809 in Georgia
7th	James JACKSON - b. (1760-1770) in Kentucky - d. Nov. 1833 in St. Helena Parish, Louisiana
6th	Thomas W. BRIDGES – b. 1795-1798 in Kentucky - d. 1880+ in Mississippi
5th	William Lee BRIDGES – b. 1829 in St. Helena Parish, La. – d. Nov. 14, 1890-Married Pauline Ann TRAVIS – b. Jan. 26, 1834 in Amite County, Miss. – d. August 3, 1911 in St. Helena Parish (buried in Jackson Cemetery, La.)
4th	Cannon W. BRIDGES – b. March, 1851 (1848 on tombstone)-d. 1923 in St. Helena Parish, La. - Buried in Jackson Cemetery in St. Helena Parish, La.
3rd	Mary Alline BRIDGES – b. August 11, 1914 – d. Sept. 8, 1990 married to Marvin Mangum Magee (July 18, 1908-Jan. 6, 1971
2nd	Dr. Derry David Magee - b. July 5, 1934 married Gwendora Wilkes -b. Sept. 1, 1936
1st	Juanita Elaine MAGEE - b. May 3, 1953 married to Steven Winslow Johnson - b. Sept. 2, 1952- Their children:

Jennifer Jean Johnson (b. Mar.16, 1978)

William Derry "Bill" Johnson (Feb. 10, 1980) m. Kellye Danielle Staudt (b. May 21, 1982)Children:
        Mia Mckenzie Johnson - b. Jan.17, 2008
        William Chase Johnson - b. Dec. 20, 2010

Ross Melvin Johnson - b. Oct. 29, 1991

B. Dora's Great-Grandparents and Grandparents

WILKES ANCESTORS

(Wilkes ancestors began in England)

The origin of the family name WILKES is conjectural as far as can be ascertained. Primitive names originated soon after the origin of the language, and for thousands of years thereafter first or given names were the only designations that men and women bore. Surnames came into being about one thousand years ago. They were introduced into England by the Normans, but it was not until the twelfth century that hereditary names became common in England and they were not universal as late as 1445. The present day spelling WILKES dates from about 1500 developing gradually from the Anglo-Saxon form spelt correcting Gaelic to an invariabale WILKYS (pronounced WILKES). The forms WILKES and WILKS are found in English records since about 1500, with WILKES predominating.

FRANCES WILKES was the father of THOMAS WILKES. Frances died in Edgecombe County. North Carolina, in May, 1745. He was married to Grace Wilkes.

THOMAS WILKES' birth date and place has not been established after extensive research. Most likely he was born in 1735. About 1762, he married Mary Conyers, daughter of Richard and Margaret Arundel. The five known children were: Reuben Wilkes, ABNER WILKES, Francis Wilkes, Richard Wilkes, and William Wilkes. It has been assumed that Thomas died between 1808-1810 and Mary died between 1800 and the taking of the 1810 census.

ABNER WILKES, son of Thomas and Mary (Conyers) Wilkes, was born about 1766 in North Carolina. He married Martha Crider about 1784-6. His second marriage was to Jerusha Brown of South Carolina.

JOHN B. (Brown) WILKES, son of Abner and Jerusha Brown Wilkes was born in Marion County, MS on March 8, 1819. He married Oney Rebecca Pritchard in Copiah County on January 19, 1841. Oney Rebecca was born March 20, 1823, the daughter of John and Elizabeth Pritchard. In 1842, John and family moved to Claiborne Parish, LA and settled about five miles south of Homer, LA. Due to serious illness, they had to disperse their holdings among their children who had to go live with family members. John died of cancer on April 25, 1860. Oney Rebecca Wilkes died January 25, 1858.

SAMUEL WARREN WILKES was born on May 15, 1849 and died on July 8, 1918. He built in 1896 and co-owned the "Carrie B" which transported cotton and general merchandise between New Orleans, La. and Columbia, Miss. He married Vandellia Dorcas McMillan on February 2, 1870. Vandellia was born on January 27, 1849, the daughter of Adolphus H. McMillan and Angelina Bateman. After a few years of marriage, they left Angie, La. and move to the Fairview Plantation in St. Francisville, LA.

LUCION WILKES was born on June 23, 1884 at St. Francisville, La. He married Lavanda Armentha Morris on January 13, 1907 at Mt. Hermon, La. Lucion died on August 10, 1952 and Lavanda died on February 13, 1971. Both are buried in the Mt. Pisgah Baptist Church Cemetery.

EARL SAMUEL WILKES was born on Feb. 5, 1912 and died on January 29, 1994. He married Willie Marie Burch, daughter of Arthur W. Burch and Mary Jemima Foil, on Oct. 4, 1934. Willie was born on Jan. 30, 1915 and died on Jan. 8, 2002. Both are buried in the Mt. Pisgah Baptist Church Cemetery.

GWENDORA WILKES MAGEE was born on Sept. 1, 1936 and married Derry David Magee on October 11, 1952. Derry was born on July 5, 1934 to Marvin Mangum Magee and Mary Alline Bridges Magee. Gwendora and Derry have one daughter, JUANITA ELAINE MAGEE, born on May 3, 1953. She married Steven Winslow Johnson who was born on Sept. 2, 1952. They have three children: Jennifer Jean Johnson, William Derry "Bill" Johnson, and Ross Melvin Johnson.

William Derry "Bill" Johnson married Kellye Danielle Staudt on July 23, 2005 in Nashville, TN. They have a daughter Mia Mckenzie Johnson, born on January 17, 2008 and a son William Chase Johnson, born on December 20, 2010. Both were born in Nashville, TN.

MORRIS ANCESTORS

SIMEON (SIMON) MORRIS
(Born in 1794 in S.C.)

ELIZABETH SMITH
(Born in 1790 in N.C.)

JAMES WASHINGTON MORRIS
(Nov. 19, 1835-Jan. 1, 1922)

FRANCES JANE ALFORD
(Aug. 20, 1838-Jan. 25, 1929)

JAMES ALEXANDER MORRIS
(May 18, 1864- June 29, 1936)

FANNIE ELIZABETH OTT
(July, 1872-Sept. 25, 1900)

LAVANDA ARMENTHA MORRIS
(Aug. 7, 1890-Feb. 13, 1971)

LUCION WILKES
(June 23, 1884-Aug. 10, 1953)

EARL SAMUEL WILKES, SR.
(Feb. 5, 1912-Jan. 29, 1994)

WILLIE MARIE BURCH
(Jan. 30, 1915-Jan. 8, 2002)

GWENDORA WILKES
(Sept. 1, 1936)

DERRY DAVID MAGEE
(July 5, 1934)

JUANITA ELAINE MAGEE
(May 3, 1953)

STEVEN W. JOHNSON
(Sept. 2, 1952)

Their children:
Jennifer Jean Johnson

(b. Mar. 16, 1978)

William Derry "Bill" Johnson
married Kellye Danielle Staudt

(b. Feb. 10, 1980)
(b. May 21, 1982)

Their children:
Mia Mckenzie Johnson(b. Jan. 17, 2008)
William Chase Johnsonb. Dec. 20, 2010)

Ross Melvin Johnson(b. Oct. 29, 1991)

MORRIS ANCESTORS

WILLIAM MORRIS
(b. abt. 1730 in S.C.)

BENJAMIN MORRIS
(b. abt. 1763 in S.C.)

(The draft version of the Morris family genealogy indicates that the relationship between William and Benjamin is tentative.)

SIMON MORRIS	ELIZABETH SMITH
(Born in 1794 in S.C.)	(Born in 1790 in N.C.)
Their children were:	
Valinda Morris	b. June 19, 1819 -Pike County, MS)
Elkanah L. "Canie" Morris	b. abt. 1827
Pinkney T. Morris	b. abt. 1828
Salena C. Morris	b. abt. 1932 in Pike County, Miss.

JAMES WASHINGTON MORRIS	FRANCES JANE ALFORD
(Nov. 19, 1835-Jan. 1, 1922)	(Aug. 20, 1838-Jan. 25, 1929)

James Washington Morris whose nickhame was "Wash" and wife Frances Jane Alford are both buried in the Oscar Morris Cemetery, Highway 1055, Mt. Hermon, LA. "Wash's" children listed in the 1880 census were:

Oscar Elonzo Morris	b. May 25, 1860d. April 15, 1941
Seaborn Simon Morris	b. May 23, 1862d. Aug. 4, 1924)
JAMES ALEXANDER MORRIS	b. May 18, 1864d. June 29, 193
Harmon Galmore Morris	b. 1866
Almon Melton Morris	b. Feb. 13, 1867d. Sept. 17, 1948
William H. Morris	b. 1868 in La.
*Ophalier Morris	(April 14, 1876 - Jan. 27, 1935)

*1880 Census lists her as Margaret Ophalier Morris

JAMES ALEXANDER MORRIS	FANNIE ELIZABETH OTT
(May 18, 1864-June 29, 1936)	(July 22, 1871-Sept. 25, 1900)

Upon the death of James Alexander Morris' first wife Fannie Elizabeth Ott, he was left with three children to raise: Lavanda, age 10, Eldridge Reid 9, and Fannie 13 days old. Evidently, Fannie Elizabeth died of childbirth complications since she died 13 days after giving birth to Fannie. According to the Mt. Hermon Cemetery records, Fannie Elizabeth Ott Morris and their infant born on Feb. 23, 1892, who died at birth are buried there in unmarked graves. We have not been able to locate James Alexander's grave at this time.

According to the marriage license, James Alexander Morris married Miss Evie Barker on January 2, 1902 in Washington Parish, Louisiana with the ceremony being performed by E. Banister, J.P. James Alexander Morris and Evie Barker Morris had one daughter Mabel Morris who was born in 1909 and died July 9, 1945.

After James Alexander's death in 1936, Evie purchased lots in Bogalusa from Jim Richardson. In a land transfer on Dec. 23, 1938, it is recorded that Evie Barker Morris purchased Lots Twenty One (21) and Twenty Two (22) of Block Twenty Two (22) in the City of Bogalusa, La. Recorded in the Bogalusa Daily News on Monday, July 9, 1945, Mabel Morris Brock Walker, her mother Evie Barker Morris, and Mabel's present husband, James Walker, were killed in a violent domestic murder on July 9, 1945 in Bogalusa, La., by Mabel's ex-husband, Jimmy Brock, who was on parole from prison. Jealousy was found to be the motive in the triple slaying and Brock's suicide. (Copies of the newspaper articles reporting these murders are in the Morris notebook compiled by Derry and Gwendora Magee, 2010.)

Notes written by Jessie Lee Simpson:

"James Washington Morris married Frances Jane Alford (Jep's sister) and lived with their five sons in a log cabin on Silver Creek about a quarter of a mile north of the Grace home. They had Oscar, born in 1860, then Simeon Seaborn, James Alexander, Harmon Galmarie, and Almon Melton. While his sons were still young, "Wash" left his family and took up with one of the Grace girls, Mahalia, moved up the creek another quarter of a mile and built another log cabin. They had three children: William H.

Morris, Ophelia (Ophalier) Morris, and William who died young. This made four log houses along Silver Creek with about a quarter of a mile between each one. The last house Cousin Wash built is still standing and is owned by his great granddaughter and husband, Evelyn Morris and Esco Riley. They use it for a hay barn. My son-in-law, Buddy Alford, was born in this house."

ARTHUR WILMER BURCH AND MARY JEMIMA FOIL
(Married August 6, 1905)

Arthur Wilmer Burch was born on July 17, 1873 to John Richard Burch, Jr. (Jan. 9, 1832-Jan. 15, 1914) and Melissa L. Brumfield (Oct. 22, 1843-June 7, 1923). (Dates according to tombstones.) JOHN R. BURCH, JR. and MELISSA L. BRUMFIELD had the following 11 children:

1. Lena Leota Burch (July 23, 1864-Jan. 28, 1952) married Steven Pinkney Richardson (Dec. 24, 1849-May 6, 1907). They had twelve children: Ella, Alice, Hammond, Hazel, Rosa, John, Elise, Walton, Anita, Frank, Lamar, and infant daughter.
2. William V. Burch was born on July 22, 1865. He married Floy Simmons. They had two children: Allie and Murphy J.
3. Walter V. Burch was born Aug. 17, 1866 and died April 2, 1942. He married Deliliah Miller (Oct. 11, 1880-June 2, 194?
4. Frances Clotena Burch was born on Oct. 14, 1868. She married Willie Alford. They had one daughter, Melissa Alford
5. Mary Rebecca Burch was born on Oct. 27, 1869 and married to John Alford. They had one son, Emon Alford
6. Oscar Monroe was born on Aug. 17, 1871 and married a Mrs. Ezell.
7. ARTHUR WILMER BURCH was born on July 17, 1873 and died on March 14, 1948. (tombstone) He was married August 6, 1905 to Mary Jemima Foil born on June 7, 1883 and died on Sept. 16, 1971. They had ten children: Lewis B. Burch was born Dec. 30, 1874
8. Rosa A. Burch was born July 17, 1876
9. J. Weston Burch was born June 13, 1878
10. Thomas Burch was born Aug. 27, 1879

ARTHUR WILMER BURCH (July 17, 1873-March 14, 1948 and MARY JEMIMA FOIL BURCH (June 7, 1883-September 16, 1971 had ten children. Arthur lived to be 75 years of age, and Mary Jemima lived to be 88 years old.

1. Vivian Irene Burch (Sept. 15, 1906-Oct. 23, 1998)
2. Milford Henry Burch, single (Jan. 14, 1908-Feb. 28, 1970)
3. Hazel Gladys Burch (Sept. 28, 1909-Nov. 26, 1949)
4. Wilson Edwin Burch (Mar. 11, 1911-April 25,1991)
5. Clara Mae Burch (Feb. 23, 1913-August, 1987)
6. WILLIE MARIE BURCH(Jan. 30, 1915-Jan. 8, 2002)
7. Arthur Wilmer Burch, Jr. (Dec. 12, 1916-Oct. 4, 1992)
8. Irma Lee Burch (April 17, 1919-May 14, 1985)
9. Dorman Paul Burch (Aug. 24, 1921-May 17, 2003)
10. Donald John Burch (May 24, 1929-Nov. 16, 2002)

WILLIE MARIE BURCH married EARL SAMUEL WILKES, SR. on October 6, 1934. They had eight children:

1. Bobbie Earl Wilkes (b. Jan. 15, 1935)
2. GWENDORA WILKES (b. Sept. 1, 1936)
3. Dorothy Elaine Wilkes (b. May 5, 1938)
4. Infant son (Dec. 23, 1940-Dec. 23, 1940)
5. Faye Ellen Wilkes (b. April 12, 1944)
6. Janice Marie Wilkes (b. Sept. 29, 1946)
7. Kathy Wilkes (Sept. 25, 1951-Apr. 2, 1994)
8. Earl Samuel (Chuck) Wilkes, Jr. (b. Jan. 27, 1953)

GWENDORA WILKES married DERRY DAVID MAGEE on October 11, 1952. Derry was born on July 5, 1934 to Marvin Mangum Magee and Mary Alline Bridges. Gwendora and Derry have one daughter JUANITA ELAINE MAGEE born on May 3, 1953.

JUANITA ELAINE MAGEE born on May 3, 1953, and married on August 11, 1972, in Kentwood, La. to STEVEN WINSLOW JOHNSON, born in Houston, TX on Sept. 2, 1952, oldest son of Arta Elmer Johnson and Betty Jean Henderson.

They have three children: Jennifer Jean Johnson, b. Mar. 16, 1978; WILLIAM DERRY "BILL" JOHNSON, b. Feb. 10, 1980; and Ross Melvin Johnson, b. Oct. 29, 1991.

WILLIAM DERRY "BILL" JOHNSON, b. Feb. 10, 1980 in Flowood, Miss., married Kellye Danielle Staudt on July 23, 2005. Kellye was born in Nashville, TN on May 21, 1982 to Daniel Eric Staudt and Vonda Joan Mann who were married on April 14, 1973. Bill and Kellye have one daughter and one son:

MIA MCKENZIE JOHNSON b. Jan. 17, 2008, in Nashville, TN

WILLIAM CHASE JOHNSON b. Dec. 20, 2010, in Nashville, TN

JAMES L. FOYLE

JAMES L. FOYLE was born about 1700, most likely in England, and died most likely in North Carolina in 1771. The ancestral home of the FOYLE'S was in Northern Ireland on the Foyle River, which is about 20 miles long and flows north between County Derry and County Donegal in Erie, North Ireland and expands into the estuary Lake Foyle.

The first record we have of them (The Foyle's) in this country is of JAMES L. FOYLE Esq., being appointed justice of peace in Onslow Co., North Carolina by Governor Gabriel Johnston in March, 1734. He was also in the assembly of the colony in 1734. In 1739 he was reappointed justice of the peace, also sheriff of Onslow Co. He continued in politics for twenty years or more and there is a record of his collecting funds as sheriff in 1753-54. He died in Onslow Co., North Carolina in 1771.

JAMES L. FOYLE came to the Continent when quite young, being a man of ability and willing to serve his country in any capacity or office in America. A copy of JAMES L. FOYLE'S will is in the FOYLE Genealogy book compiled by Zuma Fendlason Magee along with an exact copy of his appointment as is on record in the Department of Archives and History in North Carolina.

In JAMES L. FOYLE'S will which was written in 1771, he left his son, James Foyle, Jr., 343 acres, his son, JOHN FOYLE, 343 acres with the two dividing equally the cattle and working tools belonging to the plantation. He and his wife had four children: James Jr., John, Elizabeth, and Charity. His daughter, Elizabeth, was willed James' negro woman named Rose and other household furniture and items. His daughter, Charity, was willed his negro man named Sam, his black mare and household furniture and items.

Whether or not, LT. JOHN FOYLE married in North Carolina or after he came to Georgia, we have not been able to find out. After the search of land grants of Georgia, we do find that he was owner of large plantations in both Lee and Morgan Counties, by the time of the Revolutionary War. And we feel certain that the schooling which his father JAMES FOYLE refers to qualified him for responsible places.

LT. JOHN FOIL (a Revolutionary Soldier) and MARY FOIL were the parents of two sons, WILLIAM FOIL and Robert and three daughters, Mary Foyle Allison, one who married William Peel, and another who married John Peel. (Lt. John Foyle died in Morgan County, Georgia in 1815. His wife Mary died in 1827.)

The outstanding provision in LT. JOHN FOYLE'S will, written in 1815, is the emphasis on his children adhering to his religious beliefs. In order to understand it, we now know something of the history of Ireland. Northern Ireland, the ancestral home of the FOYLE'S was settled mostly by Protestants from England and Scotland. There was constant friction between the new settlers and the Catholic population. In 1641 the persecution of the Protestants reached its height when many were put to death. This persecution continued until 1690 when William III of England came to the throne. He was protestant, so persecution of the Catholic began and continued for more than a century. The Catholics were forbidden, under the penalty of death, to attend their church or to rear their children up in the Catholic faith. Such a background naturally was a breeder of religious prejudice which took generations of religious freedom to erase.

LT. JOHN FOYLE'S beloved wife was willed the choice of furniture, one of the best cows, and a comfortable and sufficient support out of his estate annually during her natural life. He willed WILLIAM FOIL forty acres of land, spring and house, and all of his bodily clothing with all his plantation and mechanical work tools—Brow self Interpreting Bible Watson body of divinity of Westminister confession of faith. The remainder of his land was willed to be divided between William Peel, John Peel, and Robert Foyle.

WILLIAM FOIL and his wife Sarah were both born in Georgia in 1783. After John's father's estate was settled, he sold his property in Georgia and moved to Mississippi. The 1820 census lists them as living in Mississippi, and the 1830 census lists them as living in Louisiana, Washington Parish. The 1850 census lists them as living in Pike County, Miss. where William was a preacher. They are buried in the Foil Cemetery about 12 miles above Tylertown, Miss. in Walthall County. They had eight children: Polly Ann, Robert, William Foil, Jr., Jane, Sarah Mary, Angeline, Caroline, and JOHN C. FOIL.

JOHN C. FOIL (1824-1880) was the eighth child of William and Sarah Foil, both born in 1783 in Georgia. He married Mary Ann Buckhalter (1835-1917), and they had the following children: WILLIAM HENRY FOIL, David F. Foil, Johnnie R. Foil, Thomas D. Foil, Mary Theresa Foil, Jacob Carter Foil, and Howard Vier Foil.

WILLIAM HENRY FOIL was born on Jan. 1, 1874 and died April 4, 1930. He married in 1872 Clara Belle Wood who was born on Jan. 8, 1856 and died May 9, 1927. They were the parents of nine children: Edgar Foil, Elmer Foil, Alba Foil, MARY JEMIMA FOIL, William Ezra Foil, Eva Gertrude Foil, Thomas Edward Foil, Ernest Foil, and Henry Foil.

MARY JEMIMA FOIL was born on June 7, 1883 and died on Sept. 16, 1971 (tombstone). On August 6, 1905 she married Arthur Wilmer Burch who was born on July 17, 1873 and died on March 14, 1948 (tombstone). Both are buried in the Mt. Pisgah Baptist Cemetery. They were the parents of ten children: Vivian Irene, Milford Henry, Hazel Gladys, Wilson Edwin, Clara Mae, WILLIE MARIE BURCH, Arthur Wilmer Burch, Jr., Irma Lee, Dorman Paul, and Donald John.

WILLIIE MARIE BURCH was born on Jan. 30, 1915 and died on Jan. 8, 2002. She married Earl Samuel Wilkes, Sr. on October 6, 1934. Earl was born on February 5, 1912 and died on Jan. 29, 1994. They had eight children: Bobbie Earl, GWENDORA, Dorothy Elaine, Infant son, Faye Ellen, Janice Marie, Kathy, and Earl Samuel Wilkes, Jr.

GWENDORA WILKES was born on September 1, 1936. She married on October 11, 1952 Derry David Magee who was born on July 5, 1934 to Marvin Mangum Magee and Mary Alline Bridges Magee. They had one daughter:

JUANITA ELAINE MAGEE was born on May 3, 1953. She married Steven Winslow Johnson on August 11, 1972. They have three children: Jennifer Jean Johnson (b. March 16, 1978), William Derry "Bill" Johnson (b. Feb. 10, 1980), and Ross Melvin Johnson (b. Oct. 29, 1991).

WILLIAM DERRY "BILL" JOHNSON   KELLYE DANIELLE STAUDT
(b. Feb. 10, 1980)   (m. July 23, 2005)   (b. May 21, 1982)

Bill and Kellye have one daughter, Mia Mckenzie Johnson born in Nashville, TN on January 17, 2008 and a son William Chase Johnson born in Nashville, TN on December 20, 2010.

OTT ANCESTORS

Jacob Ott was born in Switzerland in latter part of 17th Century and married Gretchen Schmitts (or Gertrude Schmitzer). He emigrated to America near the middle of the 18th Century and settled in Orangeburg District, South Carolina. He obtained South Carolina Royal Land Grants:

1771	200 acres on Edisto River
1772	50 acres
1773	50 acre

JACOB OTT II   (b. abt. 1703/1708)

Jacob emigrated to America near the middle of the 18th Century and settled in Orangeburg District, South Carolina. Jacob Ott II married Margaret Fichtner in Orangeburg in 1754.

JACOB OTT III   MARGARET JACKSON
(1774*-1836)   (1797-)

According to the Ott history book, Jacob Ott III was born in Orangeburg, S.C. in 1755 and died in 1836 at Mt. Hermon, La.

*According to the Mt. Hermon Cemetery records, he was born in 1774. He is buried in the family cemetery located in what is now Washington Parish, La. This cemetery was near his home site in Washington Parish. This cemetery has long been abandoned. Since the graves of family members were not marked, there is no way to identify the persons buried here.

Jacob Ott III married Margaret Jackson in Orangeburg District, South Carolina in 1797. They were married by a Justice of the Peace. According to Margaret Jackson Ott's sworn statement, there is no public nor private record of the marriage.

Jacob Ott III emigrated to Louisiana in 1807. He first settled a Spanish grant near what is now Amite, La. Later, about 1812, he moved to the Burch Headright in Washington Parish. Later, he moved to the Busby Headright, located about two miles north of Mt. Hermon, La. There he died in 1836. Jacob Ott III had a son,

JOEL OTT, whose mother is unknown. Joel was born in 1782 and died in 1879.

Children of Jacob Ott III and Margaret Jackson Ott of Louisiana included:

Isaac Ott	b. 6-14-1789 (died in infancy)
Charles Ott	1799-1867
Jessie Ott	1802-1876
Naomi Ott	1805-1885
Sarah Ott	1808-1868
Samuel Ott	1811-1831
Charlotte Ott	1813-1895
Jacob Ott IV	1817-1869

JOEL OTT   (m. July 11, 1814)   MARIA CUTRER
(1782-1879)   ( )

Joel Ott was born in 1782 in South Carolina and died in Livingston Parish, La. in 1879. He is buried near Hog Branch in Livingston Parish. Joel came to Louisiana from South Carolina with his father. When Joel married Maria Cutrer on July 11, 1814, he settled on an estate near Mt. Hermon, La. where he lived until 1861. At this time, he moved to Livingston Parish, La. and settled near what is now Watson, La. He and Maria had nine children. Maria died, and he later married Ascitheca (Acineth 1850 Census spelling) Wallace of Monticello, Miss. Joel Ott and Ascitheca Wallace had a son Thomas born in 1838 who was killed in the Civil War. He was listed as a Lieutenant in service.

In 1850 Census records, Joel Ott and (Acineth) Ott had 11 people living in their household. Two of his children by Maria Cutrer, LAWRENCE W. OTT (19 years old) and Rachel Ott (17 years old), were living with him and his second wife, Ascitheca Wallace Ott. An additional eight children were enumerated in Joel's household along with Mirian Small, age 21 in this census report. (Get complete list of children from the *Ott History Book*. We only have a few pages of the book.)

JOEL and MARIA CUTRER OTT'S children were:

Jephtha Ott	b. 1815
Joseph Ott	b. 1819
Jacob Ott	b. 1821
Charles Ott	b. 1823
Dehlia Ott	b. 1825
Elizabeth Ott	b. 1828
George Ott	b. 1829
LAWRENCE OTT	b. 1831 d. 1885
Rachael Ott	b. 1833

LAWRENCE W. OTT   SOPHIA E. STEVENS
(1831-1885)   ( )

Lawrence was born in South Carolina and the eighth child of Joel Ott and Maria Cutrer Ott. He is buried in the old Joel Ott Cemetery on the old Joel Ott place at Mt. Hermon. Lawrence married Sophia E. Stevens who was born in North Carolina. In the 1860 Census records, Lawrence was 29 years old and Maria was 17 years old. There were no additional people living in Lawrence's household at this time. In the 1870 and 1880 census records, Lawrence and Sophia had the following children:

1870 Census	Margaret L. Ott	10 years
	Minerva E. Ott	7 years
	Mary G. Ott	1868-1906 (3 years)

1880 Census included these three:

	FANNIE E. OTT	8 years
	Georgie A. Ott	6 years
	Laura L. Ott	1975 (1 year)

FANNIE ELIZABETH OTT m. 1891 JAMES ALEXANDER MORRIS
(July 22, 1871-Sept. 25, 1900)   (May 18, 1864-June 29, 1936)

Their children were:

LAVANDA ARMENTHA MORRIS	b. Aug. 7, 1890	d. Feb. 13, 1971
Eldridge Reid Morris	b. Oct. 1891	d.
Infant Morris	b. Feb. 23, 1892	d. Oct. 13, 1892
Fannie Morris	b. Sept.12, 1900	d. Aug. 6, 1987

Fannie Elizabeth and infant Morris born on Feb. 23, 1892 and died on Oct. 13, 1892 are buried in the Mt. Hermon Cemetery at Mt. Hermon, La.

LAVANDA ARMENTHAMORRIS   LUCION WILKES
(Aug. 7, 1890-Feb. 13, 1971)(m. Jan. 13, 1907)(June 23, 1884-Aug. 10, 1953)

They were married Jan. 13, 1907 and are both buried in the Mt. Pisgah Baptist Church Cemetery, Washington Parish, La.

Their children were:

Iris Oney Wilkes	b. 1907	d. 1983
Lennie Louvenia	b. 1910	d. 1984
EARL SAMUEL WILKES	b. 1912	d. 1994
Connie Mae Wilkes	b. 1914	d. 1996
Harris Doyle Wilkes	b. 1916	d. 1985
Althea Evelyn Wilkes	b. 1918	d. 1996
Sedgie Wilson Wilkes	b. 1920	d. 1986
Elaine Delle Wilkes	b. 1922	d. 1996
Lucion Willard Wilkes	b. 1924	d. 1986

EARL SAMUEL WILKES   WILLIE MARIE BURCH
(Feb. 5, 1912-Jan. 29, 1994)   (Jan. 30, 1915-Jan. 8, 2002)

Earl Samuel Wilkes was born on February 5, 1912 and died on January 29, 1994. He was the third child and first son of Lucion Wilkes and Lavanda Armentha Morris. On October 4, 1934, Earl married Willie Marie Burch who was born on January 30, 1915 and died on January 8, 2002. Both were members of the Mt. Pisgah Baptist Church and are buried in the Mt. Pisgah Baptist Church Cemetery. Willie was the daughter of Arthur Wilson Burch and Mary Jemima Foil of the Mt. Pisgah Community. They had eight children:

Bobbie Earl Wilkes	b. January 15, 1935
GWENDORA WILKES	b. September 1, 1936
Dorothy Elaine Wilkes	b. May 5, 1938
Infant Wilkes	(Dec. 23, 1940- Dec. 23, 1940)
Faye Ellen Wilkes	b. Apr. 12, 1944
Janice Marie Wilkes	b. Sept. 29, 1946

Kathy Wilkes   (Sept. 25, 1951-April 2, 1994)
Earl Samuel "Chuck" Wilkes Jr .   b. Jan. 27, 1953

GWENDORA WILKES

Gwendora Wilkes was the second daughter and second child of Earl Samuel Wilkes and Willie Marie Burch. Gwendora was born on September 1, 1936 and married on October 11, 1952 to Derry David Magee. Derry was born on July 5, 1934 to Marvin Mangum Magee and Mary Alline Bridges. Gwendora and Derry had one daughter, Juanita Elaine Magee, who was born on May 3, 1953.

JUANITA ELAINE MAGEE

Juanita Elaine Magee, daughter of Derry and Gwendora Magee, was born on May 3, 1953 and married on August 11, 1972 to Steven Winslow Johnson at Kentwood, La. Steven was born on September 2, 1952 to Arta Elmer "Bill" Johnson and Betty Jean Henderson. Juanita and Steven had three children:

Jennifer Jean Johnson   b. March 16, 1978
William Derry "Bill" Johnson   b. February 10, 1980
Ross Melvin Johnson   b. October 29, 1991

WILLIAM DERRY "BILL" JOHNSON

William Derry "Bill" Johnson was born on February 10, 1980 in Flowood, Miss. to Steven Winslow Johnson and Juanita Elaine Magee. Bill married Kellye Danielle Staudt on July 23, 2005 at the Wight Chapel, Vanderbilt University, Nashville, TN. Kellye was born on May 21, 1982 in Nashvillle, TN to Daniel Eric Staudt and Vonda Joan Mann. Bill and Kellye have two children:

Mia Mckenzie Johnson was born on January 17, 2008, and William Chase Johnson was born on December 20, 2010 in Nashville, TN

C. Family Trees

Pedigree Chart - Derry David Magee

Chart no. _____
No. 1 on this chart is the same as no. _____ on chart no. _____

				32 Solomon Magee
			16 Willis Sims Magee	
			b: 2 Jul 1818	33 Elizabeth Weathersby
		8 Robert Solomon Magee	d: 14 Aug 1883	
		b: 2 Mar 1845		34
		p:	17 Mary Norward	
		m: abt 1865	b:	35
4 Derry David Magee	p:	d:	
b: 20 May 1866	d: 3 Dec 1888		36 Arthur C. Mangum
p: Mississippi, Simpson County	p:	18 Arthur Mangum	
m: 23 Aug 1903		b: abt 1820	37 Penelope A. Butler
p:	9 Eugenia Elizabeth Mangum	d: 20 Sep 1858	
d: 27 Oct 1929	b: 12 Nov 1846		38
p:	p: Simpson Co? Smith Co?	19 Elizabeth T. Caraway	
2 Marvin Mangum Magee	d: 3 Mar 1927	b: 1830	39
b: 18 Jul 1908	p: Simpson Co? Covington Co?	d: 20 Sep	

2 Marvin Mangum Magee
b: 18 Jul 1908
p: Collins, Mississippi
m: 25 Oct 1931
p: Collins, Miss.
d: 6 Jan 1971
p: Amite county, Miss.

			40 John Easterling
		20 Henry W. Easterling	
		b: abt 1833	41 Elizabeth Grantham
	10 John Calvin Easterling	d:	
	b: 4 Nov 1856		42
	p:	21 Mary McDonald	
	m:	b: abt 1830	43
5 Zora Easterling	p:	d:	
b: 19 Jul 1884	d: 30 Apr 1931		44
p: Jones County, Mississippi	p:	22 John Dees	
d: 21 May 1921		b:	45
p:	11 Susan Dees	d:	
	b: 5 Nov 1858		46
	p:	23 Elizabeth Miller	
	d: 3 Mar 1943	b:	47
	p:	d:	

1 Derry David Magee
b: 5 Jul 1934
p: New Orleans, Louisiana
m: 11 Oct 1952
p: Mt.Hermon, Louisiana
d:
p:

sp: Gwendora Wilkes Magee

			48 Wiley Bridges
		24 Thomas William Bridges	
		b: 1796	49 Jenny Strickland
	12 William Lee Bridges	d:	
	b: 23 Dec 1829		50
	p: St, Helena Parish, Louisiana	25 Elizabeth Jackson	
	m: 11 Jun 1850	b: 4 Jun 1800	51
	p: St. Helena Parish, La.	d: 5 Jun 1885	
6 Cannon Wilson Bridges	d: 14 Nov 1890		52
b: 22 Mar 1852	p: St, Helena Parish, Louisiana	26 William Travis	
p:		b:	53
m: 6 Mar 1906	13 Pauline Ann Travis	d:	
p:	b: 26 Jan 1831		54
d: Dec 1923	p: Amite county, Miss.	27 Nancy Hurst	
p:	d: 3 Aug 1911	b:	55
	p: St. Helena Parish, La.	d:	

3 Mary Alline Bridges
b: 22 Aug 1914
p: Liberty, Miss. (?)
d: 16 Sep 1990
p: Hammond, La.

			56 Peter Bankston
		28 Boleyn Bankston	
		b: 9 Nov 1816	57 Tabitha Robertson
	14 Thomas Jefferson Bankston	d: 4 Feb 1880	
	b: 20 Dec 1856		58 Enoch Courtney
	p:	29 Eliza Jane Courtney	
	m: 5 Dec 1877	b: 7 Mar 1825	59 Mary Ann Humble
	p:	d: 17 Feb 1863	
7 Juanita Rivers Bankston	d: 7 Sep 1942		60
b: 15 Jul 1885	p:	30	
p:		b:	61
d: 5 Oct 1965	15 Mary Elizabeth Vernon	d:	
p:	b: 2 Feb 1858		62
	p:	31	
	d:	b:	63
	p: April 17, 1898	d:	

170

Pedigree Chart - Gwendora Wilkes "Dora" Magee

Chart no. _____
No. 1 on this chart is the same as no. _____ on chart no. _____

32 Abner Wilkes

16 John B. Wilkes
b: 8 Mar 1819
d: 25 Apr 1860

33 Jerusha Brown

8 Samuel Warren Wilkes
b: 15 May 1849
p: Homer, Louisiana
m: 2 Feb 1870
p: F.M. Forbs Home, Angie , La.
d: 8 Jul 1918
p: Angie, Louisiana

34 John Pritchard

17 Oney Rebecca Pritchard
b: 20 Mar 1823
d: 25 Jan 1858

35 Elizabeth ????

4 Lucion Wilkes
b: 23 Jun 1884
p: St Francisville, Louisiana
m: 13 Jan 1907
p: Mt. Hermon, La.
d: 10 Aug 1952
p: Mt.Hermon, Louisiana

36

18 Adolphus McMillan
b: 4 Jul 1819
d: 23 Jan 1890

37

9 Vandellia Dorcas McMillan
b: 27 Jan 1849
p:
d:
p:

38

19 Angelena (Gelina) Bateman
b: 25 Dec 1825
d: 27 Jul 1909

39

2 Earl Samuel Wilkes
b: 5 Feb 1912
p: Washington Parish, Louisiana
m: 4 Oct 1934
p: Mt.Hermon, Louisiana
d: 29 Jan 1994
p: Parish of Washington 9th ward(Mt

40 Simeon Morris

20 James Washington Morris
b: 19 Nov 1835
d: 1 Jan 1922

41 Elizabeth Smith

10 James Alexander Morris
b: May 1864
p:
m: abt 1891
p:
d: 29 Jun 1936
p:

42 John Seaborn Alford

21 Frances Jane Alford
b: 20 Aug 1838
d: 25 Jan 1929

43 Margaret Brumfield

5 Lavanda Armentha Morris
b: 7 Aug 1890
p:
d: 13 Feb 1971
p:

44 Joel Ott

22 Lawerence Ott
b: 1831
d: 1885

45 Maria Cutrer

11 Fannie Elizabeth Ott
b: 27 Jul 1872
p: Louisiana
d: 25 Sep 1900
p:

46

23 Sophie E. Stevens
b: 1843
d:

47

1 Gwendora Wilkes Magee
b: 1 Sep 1936
p: Mt. Hermon, La.
m: 11 Oct 1952
p: Mt.Hermon, Louisiana
d:
p:

sp: **Derry David Magee**

48 Richard Burch

24 John Burch Senior
b:
d: 1832–1836

49

12 John Richard Burch Junior
b: 9 Jun 1832
p:
m: 24 Apr 1863
p:
d: 15 Jan 1914
p: Burch Cemetery

50

25 Samantha Clowers
b: 22 Apr 1810
d: 1 Dec 1891

51

6 Arthur Wilmer Burch Senior
b: 17 Jul 1873
p:
m:
p:
d: 14 Mar 1948
p:

52 Ezekiel Brumfield

26 John W Brumfield
b: abt 1811
d:

53

13 Melissa L Brumfield
b: 22 Oct 1843
p: Washington Parish, Louisiana
d: 7 Jun 1923
p: Burch Cemetery

54

27 Cinderilla Brumfield
b: abt 1822
d:

55

3 Willie Marie Burch
b: 30 Jan 1915
p: Mt. Hermon, La.
d: 8 Jan 2002
p: Franklinton, Louisiana

56 William Foil

28 John C Foil
b: 1824
d: 1880

57 Sarah

14 William Henry Foil
b: 1 Jan 1852
p:
m: 1873
p:
d: 4 Apr 1930
p:

58

29 Mary Ann Burkhalter
b: 1835
d: 1917

59

7 Mary Jemima Foil
b: 7 Jun 1883
p:
d: 16 Sep 1971
p:

60

30 Johnson Wood
b: abt 1824
d:

61

15 Clara Belle Wood
b: 8 Jan 1856
p:
d: 9 May 1927
p:

62

31 A F Wood
b: abt 1835
d:

63

Pedigree Chart - Steven Winslow Johnson

Chart no. _____
No. 1 on this chart is the same as no. _____ on chart no. _____

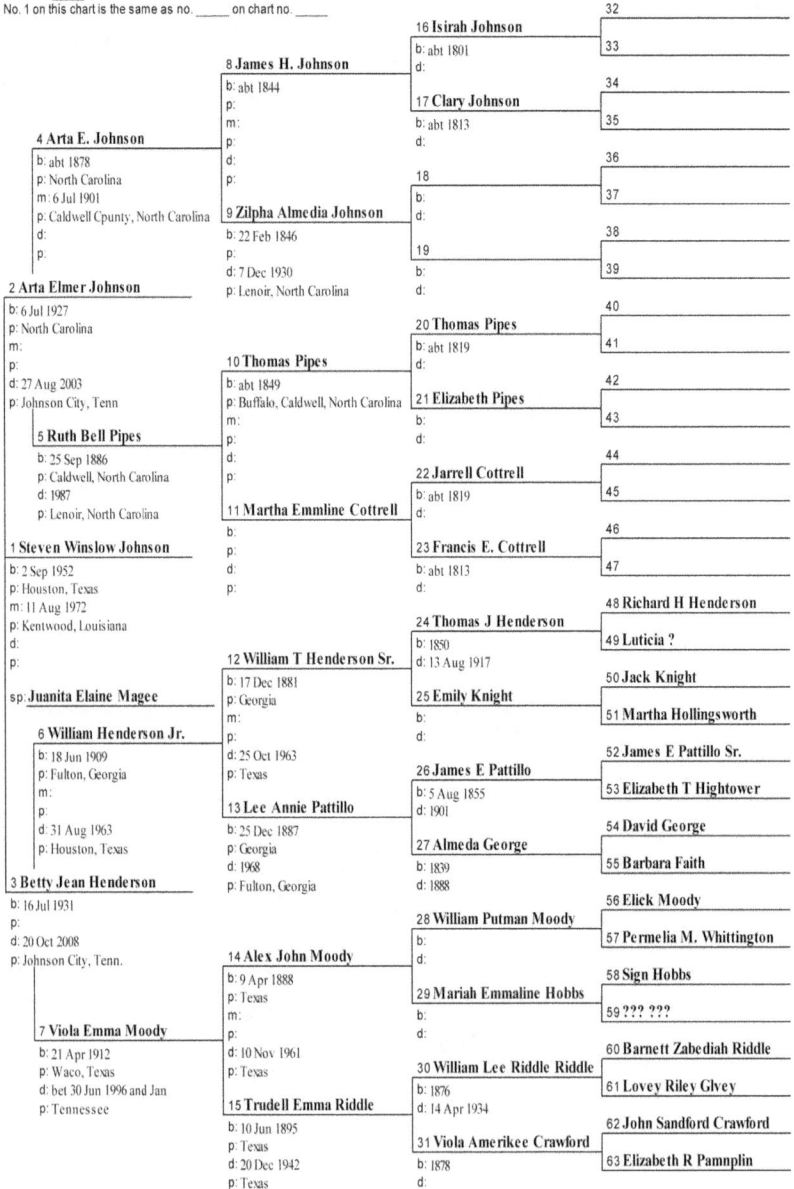

		16 Isirah Johnson b: abt 1801 d:	32 _____	
	8 James H. Johnson b: abt 1844 p: m: p: d: p:		33 _____	
		17 Clary Johnson b: abt 1813 d:	34 _____ 35 _____	
4 Arta E. Johnson b: abt 1878 p: North Carolina m: 6 Jul 1901 p: Caldwell Cpunty, North Carolina d: p:		**18** b: d:	36 _____ 37 _____	
	9 Zilpha Almedia Johnson b: 22 Feb 1846 p: d: 7 Dec 1930 p: Lenoir, North Carolina	**19** b: d:	38 _____ 39 _____	

2 Arta Elmer Johnson
b: 6 Jul 1927
p: North Carolina
m:
p:
d: 27 Aug 2003
p: Johnson City, Tenn

		20 Thomas Pipes b: abt 1819 d:	40 _____ 41 _____	
	10 Thomas Pipes b: abt 1849 p: Buffalo, Caldwell, North Carolina m: p: d: p:	**21 Elizabeth Pipes** b: d:	42 _____ 43 _____	
5 Ruth Bell Pipes b: 25 Sep 1886 p: Caldwell, North Carolina d: 1987 p: Lenoir, North Carolina		**22 Jarrell Cottrell** b: abt 1819 d:	44 _____ 45 _____	
	11 Martha Emmline Cottrell b: p: d: p:	**23 Francis E. Cottrell** b: abt 1813 d:	46 _____ 47 _____	

1 Steven Winslow Johnson
b: 2 Sep 1952
p: Houston, Texas
m: 11 Aug 1972
p: Kentwood, Louisiana
d:
p:

sp: **Juanita Elaine Magee**

		24 Thomas J Henderson b: 1850 d: 13 Aug 1917	**48 Richard H Henderson** **49 Luticia ?**	
	12 William T Henderson Sr. b: 17 Dec 1881 p: Georgia m: p: d: 25 Oct 1963 p: Texas	**25 Emily Knight** b: d:	**50 Jack Knight** **51 Martha Hollingsworth**	
6 William Henderson Jr. b: 18 Jun 1909 p: Fulton, Georgia m: p: d: 31 Aug 1963 p: Houston, Texas		**26 James E Pattillo** b: 5 Aug 1855 d: 1901	**52 James E Pattillo Sr.** **53 Elizabeth T Hightower**	
	13 Lee Annie Pattillo b: 25 Dec 1887 p: Georgia d: 1968 p: Fulton, Georgia	**27 Almeda George** b: 1839 d: 1888	**54 David George** **55 Barbara Faith**	

3 Betty Jean Henderson
b: 16 Jul 1931
p:
d: 20 Oct 2008
p: Johnson City, Tenn.

		28 William Putman Moody b: d:	**56 Elick Moody** **57 Permelia M. Whittington**	
	14 Alex John Moody b: 9 Apr 1888 p: Texas m: p: d: 10 Nov 1961 p: Texas	**29 Mariah Emmaline Hobbs** b: d:	**58 Sign Hobbs** **59 ??? ???**	
7 Viola Emma Moody b: 21 Apr 1912 p: Waco, Texas d: bet 30 Jun 1996 and Jan p: Tennessee		**30 William Lee Riddle Riddle** b: 1876 d: 14 Apr 1934	**60 Barnett Zabediah Riddle** **61 Lovey Riley Glvey**	
	15 Trudell Emma Riddle b: 10 Jun 1895 p: Texas d: 20 Dec 1942 p: Texas	**31 Viola Amerikee Crawford** b: 1878 d:	**62 John Sandford Crawford** **63 Elizabeth R Pamnplin**	

172

Pedigree Chart - Juanita Elaine Magee

Chart no. _____
No. 1 on this chart is the same as no. _____ on chart no. _____

4 Marvin Mangum Magee
b: 18 Jul 1908
p: Collins, Mississippi
m: 25 Oct 1931
p: Collins, Miss.
d: 6 Jan 1971
p: Amite county, Miss.

8 Derry David Magee
b: 20 May 1866
p: Mississippi, Simpson County
m: 23 Aug 1903
p:
d: 27 Oct 1929
p:

16 Robert Solomon Magee
b: 2 Mar 1845
d: 3 Dec 1888

32 Willis Sims Magee

33 Mary Norward

17 Eugenia Elizabeth Mangum
b: 12 Nov 1846
d: 3 Mar 1927

34 Arthur Mangum

35 Elizabeth T. Caraway

9 Zora Easterling
b: 19 Jul 1884
p: Jones County, Mississippi
d: 21 May 1921
p:

18 John Calvin Easterling
b: 4 Nov 1856
d: 30 Apr 1931

36 Henry W. Easterling

37 Mary McDonald

19 Susan Dees
b: 5 Nov 1858
d: 3 Mar 1943

38 John Dees

39 Elizabeth Miller

2 Derry David Magee
b: 5 Jul 1934
p: New Orleans, Louisiana
m: 11 Oct 1952
p: Mt.Hermon, Louisiana
d:
p:

5 Mary Alline Bridges
b: 22 Aug 1914
p: Liberty, Miss. (?)
d: 16 Sep 1990
p: Hammond, La.

10 Cannon Wilson Bridges
b: 22 Mar 1852
p:
m: 6 Mar 1906
p:
d: Dec 1923
p:

20 William Lee Bridges
b: 23 Dec 1829
d: 14 Nov 1890

40 Thomas William Bridges

41 Elizabeth Jackson

21 Pauline Ann Travis
b: 26 Jan 1831
d: 3 Aug 1911

42 William Travis

43 Nancy Hurst

11 Juanita Rivers Bankston
b: 15 Jul 1885
p:
d: 5 Oct 1965
p:

22 Thomas Jefferson Bankston
b: 20 Dec 1856
d: 7 Sep 1942

44 Boleyn Bankston

45 Eliza Jane Courtney

23 Mary Elizabeth Vernon
b: 2 Feb 1858
d:

46

47

1 Juanita Elaine Magee
b: 3 May 1953
p: Tylertown, Miss.
m: 11 Aug 1972
p: Kentwood, Louisiana
d:
p:

sp: **Steven Winslow Johnson**

6 Earl Samuel Wilkes
b: 5 Feb 1912
p: Washington Parish, Louisiana
m: 4 Oct 1934
p: Mt.Hermon, Louisiana
d: 29 Jan 1994
p: Parish of Washington 9th ward(Mt

12 Lucion Wilkes
b: 23 Jun 1884
p: St Francisville, Louisiana
m: 13 Jan 1907
p: Mt. Hermon, La.
d: 10 Aug 1952
p: Mt.Hermon, Louisiana

24 Samuel Warren Wilkes
b: 15 May 1849
d: 8 Jul 1918

48 John B. Wilkes

49 Oney Rebecca Pritchard

25 Vandellia Dorcas McMillan
b: 27 Jan 1849
d:

50 Adolphus McMillan

51 Angelena (Gelina) Bateman

13 Lavanda Armentha Morris
b: 7 Aug 1890
p:
d: 13 Feb 1971
p:

26 James Alexander Morris
b: May 1864
d: 29 Jun 1936

52 James Washington Morris

53 Frances Jane Alford

27 Fannie Elizabeth Ott
b: 27 Jul 1872
d: 25 Sep 1900

54 Lawerence Ott

55 Sophie E. Stevens

3 Gwendora Wilkes Magee
b: 1 Sep 1936
p: Mt. Hermon, La.
d:
p:

7 Willie Marie Burch
b: 30 Jan 1915
p: Mt. Hermon, La.
d: 8 Jan 2002
p: Franklinton, Louisiana

14 Arthur Burch Senior
b: 17 Jul 1873
p:
m:
p:
d: 14 Mar 1948
p:

28 John Richard Burch Junior
b: 9 Jun 1832
d: 15 Jan 1914

56 John Burch Senior

57 Samantha Clowers

29 Melissa L Brumfield
b: 22 Oct 1843
d: 7 Jun 1923

58 John W Brumfield

59 Cinderilla Brumfield

15 Mary Jemima Foil
b: 7 Jun 1883
p:
d: 16 Sep 1971
p:

30 William Henry Foil
b: 1 Jan 1852
d: 4 Apr 1930

60 John C Foil

61 Mary Ann Burkhalter

31 Clara Belle Wood
b: 8 Jan 1856
d: 9 May 1927

62 Johnson Wood

63 A F Wood

173

Pedigree Chart - Jennifer Jean Johnson

2 Steven Winslow Johnson
b: 2 Sep 1952
p: Houston, Texas
m: 11 Aug 1972
p: Kentwood, Louisiana
d:
p:

1 Jennifer Jean Johnson
b: 16 Mar 1978
p: Flowood, Misasissippi
m:
p:
d:
p:

sp:

4 Arta Elmer Johnson
b: 6 Jul 1927
p: North Carolina
m:
p:
d: 27 Aug 2003
p: Johnson City, Tenn

5 Betty Jean Henderson
b: 16 Jul 1931
p:
d: 20 Oct 2008
p: Johnson City, Tenn.

6 Derry David Magee
b: 5 Jul 1934
p: New Orleans, Louisiana
m: 11 Oct 1952
p: Mt.Hermon, Louisiana
p:

3 Juanita Elaine Magee
b: 3 May 1953
p: Tylertown, Miss.
d:
p:

7 Gwendora Wilkes Magee
b: 1 Sep 1936
p: Mt. Hermon, La.
d:
p:

8 Arta E. Johnson
b: abt 1878
p: North Carolina
m: 6 Jul 1901
p: Caldwell Cpunty, North Carolina
d:
p:

9 Ruth Bell Pipes
b: 25 Sep 1886
p: Caldwell, North Carolina
d: 1987
p: Lenoir, North Carolina

10 William Henderson Jr.
b: 18 Jun 1909
p: Fulton, Georgia
m:
p:
d: 31 Aug 1963
p: Houston, Texas

11 Viola Emma Moody
b: 21 Apr 1912
p: Waco, Texas
d: bet 30 Jun 1996 and Jan
p: Tennessee

12 Marvin Mangum Magee
b: 18 Jul 1908
p: Collins, Mississippi
m: 25 Oct 1931
p: Collins, Miss.
d: 6 Jan 1971
p: Amite county, Miss.

13 Mary Alline Bridges
b: 22 Aug 1914
p: Liberty, Miss. (?)
d: 16 Sep 1990
p: Hammond, La.

14 Earl Samuel Wilkes
b: 5 Feb 1912
p: Washington Parish, Louisiana
m: 4 Oct 1934
p: Mt.Hermon, Louisiana
d: 29 Jan 1994
p: Parish of Washington 9th ward(Mt

15 Willie Marie Burch
b: 30 Jan 1915
p: Mt. Hermon, La.
d: 8 Jan 2002
p: Franklinton, Louisiana

16 James H. Johnson
b: abt 1844
d:

17 Zilpha Almedia Johnson
b: 22 Feb 1846
d: 7 Dec 1930

18 Thomas Pipes
b: abt 1849
d:

19 Martha Emmline Cottrell
b:
d:

20 William T Henderson Sr.
b: 17 Dec 1881
d: 25 Oct 1963

21 Lee Annie Pattillo
b: 25 Dec 1887
d: 1968

22 Alex John Moody
b: 9 Apr 1888
d: 10 Nov 1961

23 Trudell Emma Riddle
b: 10 Jun 1895
d: 20 Dec 1942

24 Derry David Magee
b: 20 May 1866
d: 27 Oct 1929

25 Zora Easterling
b: 19 Jul 1884
d: 21 May 1921

26 Cannon Wilson Bridges
b: 22 Mar 1852
d: Dec 1923

27 Juanita Rivers Bankston
b: 15 Jul 1885
d: 5 Oct 1965

28 Lucion Wilkes
b: 23 Jun 1884
d: 10 Aug 1952

29 Lavanda Armentha Morris
b: 7 Aug 1890
d: 13 Feb 1971

30 Arthur Burch Senior
b: 17 Jul 1873
d: 14 Mar 1948

31 Mary Jemima Foil
b: 7 Jun 1883
d: 16 Sep 1971

32 Isirah Johnson

33 Clary Johnson

34

35

36 Thomas Pipes

37 Elizabeth Pipes

38 Jarrell Cottrell

39 Francis E. Cottrell

40 Thomas J Henderson

41 Emily Knight

42 James E Pattillo

43 Almeda George

44 William Putman Moody

45 Mariah Emmaline Hobbs

46 William Lee Riddle Riddle

47 Viola Amerikee Crawford

48 Robert Solomon Magee

49 Eugenia Elizabeth Mangum

50 John Calvin Easterling

51 Susan Dees

52 William Lee Bridges

53 Pauline Ann Travis

54 Thomas Jefferson Bankston

55 Mary Elizabeth Vernon

56 Samuel Warren Wilkes

57 Vandellia Dorcas McMillan

58 James Alexander Morris

59 Fannie Elizabeth Ott

60 John Richard Burch Junior

61 Melissa L Brumfield

62 William Henry Foil

63 Clara Belle Wood

Pedigree Chart - William Derry "Bill" Johnson

Chart no. _____
No. 1 on this chart is the same as no. _____ on chart no. _____

			32 Isirah Johnson
		16 James H. Johnson	33 Clary Johnson
		b: abt 1844	
	8 Arta E. Johnson	d:	34
	b: abt 1878	17 Zilpha Almedia Johnson	
	p: North Carolina	b: 22 Feb 1846	35
4 Arta Elmer Johnson	m: 6 Jul 1901	d: 7 Dec 1930	
b: 6 Jul 1927	p: Caldwell County, North Carolina		36 Thomas Pipes
p: North Carolina	d:	18 Thomas Pipes	
m:	p:	b: abt 1849	37 Elizabeth Pipes
p:	9 Ruth Bell Pipes	d:	
d: 27 Aug 2003	b: 25 Sep 1886		38 Jarrell Cottrell
p: Johnson City, Tenn	p: Caldwell, North Carolina	19 Martha Emmline Cottrell	
	d: 1987	b:	39 Francis E. Cottrell
2 Steven Winslow Johnson	p: Lenoir, North Carolina	d:	
b: 2 Sep 1952			40 Thomas J Henderson
p: Houston, Texas		20 William T Henderson Sr.	
m: 11 Aug 1972		b: 17 Dec 1881	41 Emily Knight
p: Kentwood, Louisiana	10 William Henderson Jr.	d: 25 Oct 1963	
d:	b: 18 Jun 1909		42 James E Pattillo
p:	p: Fulton, Georgia	21 Lee Annie Pattillo	
	m:	b: 25 Dec 1887	43 Almeda George
5 Betty Jean Henderson	p:	d: 1968	
b: 16 Jul 1931	d: 31 Aug 1963		44 William Putman Moody
p:	p: Houston, Texas	22 Alex John Moody	
d: 20 Oct 2008		b: 9 Apr 1888	45 Mariah Emmaline Hobbs
p: Johnson City, Tenn.	11 Viola Emma Moody	d: 10 Nov 1961	
1 William Derry Johnson	b: 21 Apr 1912		46 William Lee Riddle Riddle
b: 10 Feb 1980	p: Waco, Texas	23 Trudell Emma Riddle	
p: Flowood, Mississippi	d: bet 30 Jun 1996 and Jan	b: 10 Jun 1895	47 Viola Amerikee Crawford
m: 23 Jul 2005	p: Tennessee	d: 20 Dec 1942	
p: Nashville, Tenn.			48 Robert Solomon Magee
d:		24 Derry David Magee	
p:		b: 20 May 1866	49 Eugenia Elizabeth Mangum
	12 Marvin Mangum Magee	d: 27 Oct 1929	
sp: Kellye Danielle Staudt	b: 18 Jul 1908		50 John Calvin Easterling
	p: Collins, Mississippi	25 Zora Easterling	
6 Derry David Magee	m: 25 Oct 1931	b: 19 Jul 1884	51 Susan Dees
b: 5 Jul 1934	p: Collins, Miss.	d: 21 May 1921	
p: New Orleans, Louisiana	d: 6 Jan 1971		52 William Lee Bridges
m: 11 Oct 1952	p: Amite county, Miss.	26 Cannon Wilson Bridges	
p: Mt.Hermon, Louisiana		b: 22 Mar 1852	53 Pauline Ann Travis
d:	13 Mary Alline Bridges	d: Dec 1923	
p:	b: 22 Aug 1914		54 Thomas Jefferson Bankston
	p: Liberty, Miss. (?)	27 Juanita Rivers Bankston	
3 Juanita Elaine Magee	d: 16 Sep 1990	b: 15 Jul 1885	55 Mary Elizabeth Vernon
b: 3 May 1953	p: Hammond, La.	d: 5 Oct 1965	
p: Tylertown, Miss.			56 Samuel Warren Wilkes
d:		28 Lucion Wilkes	
p:		b: 23 Jun 1884	57 Vandellia Dorcas McMillan
	14 Earl Samuel Wilkes	d: 10 Aug 1952	
	b: 5 Feb 1912		58 James Alexander Morris
	p: Washington Parish, Louisiana	29 Lavanda Armentha Morris	
	m: 4 Oct 1934	b: 7 Aug 1890	59 Fannie Elizabeth Ott
7 Gwendora Wilkes Magee	p: Mt.Hermon, Louisiana	d: 13 Feb 1971	
b: 1 Sep 1936	d: 29 Jan 1994		60 John Richard Burch Junior
p: Mt. Hermon, La.	p: Parish of Washington 9th ward(M	30 Arthur Burch Senior	
d:		b: 17 Jul 1873	61 Melissa L Brumfield
p:	15 Willie Marie Burch	d: 14 Mar 1948	
	b: 30 Jan 1915		62 William Henry Foil
	p: Mt. Hermon, La.	31 Mary Jemima Foil	
	d: 8 Jan 2002	b: 7 Jun 1883	63 Clara Belle Wood
	p: Franklinton, Louisiana	d: 16 Sep 1971	

175

Pedigree Chart - Ross Melvin Johnson

Chart no. _____
No. 1 on this chart is the same as no. _____ on chart no. _____

```
                                                                    32 Isirah Johnson
                                                   16 James H. Johnson
                                                   b: abt 1844              33 Clary Johnson
                              8 Arta E. Johnson     d:
                              b: abt 1878                                   34
                              p: North Carolina     17 Zilpha Almedia Johnson
                              m: 6 Jul 1901         b: 22 Feb 1846          35
          4 Arta Elmer Johnson   p: Caldwell Cpunty, North Carolina   d: 7 Dec 1930
          b: 6 Jul 1927         d:                                          36 Thomas Pipes
          p: North Carolina     p:                  18 Thomas Pipes
          m:                                        b: abt 1849             37 Elizabeth Pipes
          p:                    9 Ruth Bell Pipes    d:
          d: 27 Aug 2003        b: 25 Sep 1886                              38 Jarrell Cottrell
          p: Johnson City, Tenn  p: Caldwell, North Carolina   19 Martha Emmline Cottrell
                                d: 1987                          b:          39 Francis E. Cottrell
  2 Steven Winslow Johnson      p: Lenoir, North Carolina        d:
  b: 2 Sep 1952                                                             40 Thomas J Henderson
  p: Houston, Texas                                 20 William T Henderson Sr.
  m: 11 Aug 1972                                    b: 17 Dec 1881          41 Emily Knight
  p: Kentwood, Louisiana        10 William Henderson Jr.   d: 25 Oct 1963
  d:                            b: 18 Jun 1909                              42 James E Pattillo
  p:                            p: Fulton, Georgia    21 Lee Annie Pattillo
                                m:                   b: 25 Dec 1887         43 Almeda George
        5 Betty Jean Henderson  p:                    d: 1968
        b: 16 Jul 1931          d: 31 Aug 1963                             44 William Putman Moody
        p:                      p: Houston, Texas    22 Alex John Moody
        d: 20 Oct 2008                               b: 9 Apr 1888         45 Mariah Emmaline Hobbs
        p: Johnson City, Tenn.  11 Viola Emma Moody   d: 10 Nov 1961
                                b: 21 Apr 1912                             46 William Lee Riddle Riddle
  1 Ross Melvin Johnson         p: Waco, Texas       23 Trudell Emma Riddle
  b: 29 Oct 1991                d: bet 30 Jun 1996 and Jan   b: 10 Jun 1895   47 Viola Amerikee Crawford
  p: Miami, Fla.                p: Tennessee          d: 20 Dec 1942
  m:                                                                        48 Robert Solomon Magee
  p:                                                 24 Derry David Magee
  d:                                                 b: 20 May 1866         49 Eugenia Elizabeth Mangum
  p:                            12 Marvin Mangum Magee   d: 27 Oct 1929
                                b: 18 Jul 1908                             50 John Calvin Easterling
  sp: _____                     p: Collins, Mississippi   25 Zora Easterling
                                m: 25 Oct 1931       b: 19 Jul 1884         51 Susan Dees
        6 Derry David Magee     p: Collins, Miss.    d: 21 May 1921
        b: 5 Jul 1934           d: 6 Jan 1971                              52 William Lee Bridges
        p: New Orleans, Louisiana   p: Amite county, Miss.   26 Cannon Wilson Bridges
        m: 11 Oct 1952                               b: 22 Mar 1852         53 Pauline Ann Travis
        p: Mt.Hermon, Louisiana  13 Mary Alline Bridges   d: Dec 1923
        d:                      b: 22 Aug 1914                             54 Thomas Jefferson Bankston
        p:                      p: Liberty, Miss. (?)   27 Juanita Rivers Bankston
                                d: 16 Sep 1990       b: 15 Jul 1885         55 Mary Elizabeth Vernon
  3 Juanita Elaine Magee        p: Hammond, La.      d: 5 Oct 1965
  b: 3 May 1953                                                             56 Samuel Warren Wilkes
  p: Tylertown, Miss.                               28 Lucion Wilkes
  d:                                                 b: 23 Jun 1884         57 Vandellia Dorcas McMillan
  p:                            14 Earl Samuel Wilkes   d: 10 Aug 1952
                                b: 5 Feb 1912                              58 James Alexander Morris
                                p: Washington Parish, Louisiana   29 Lavanda Armentha Morris
                                m: 4 Oct 1934        b: 7 Aug 1890         59 Fannie Elizabeth Ott
        7 Gwendora Wilkes Magee  p: Mt.Hermon, Louisiana   d: 13 Feb 1971
        b: 1 Sep 1936           d: 29 Jan 1994                            60 John Richard Burch Junior
        p: Mt. Hermon, La.      p: Parish of Washington 9th ward(Mt   30 Arthur Burch Senior
        d:                                           b: 17 Jul 1873         61 Melissa L Brumfield
        p:                      15 Willie Marie Burch   d: 14 Mar 1948
                                b: 30 Jan 1915                            62 William Henry Foil
                                p: Mt. Hermon, La.   31 Mary Jemima Foil
                                d: 8 Jan 2002        b: 7 Jun 1883         63 Clara Belle Wood
                                p: Franklinton, Louisiana   d: 16 Sep 1971
```

Pedigree Chart - Kellye Danielle Staudt

Chart no. _____
No. 1 on this chart is the same as no. _____ on chart no. _____

8 Howard Louis Staudt
b: abt 1900
p:
m: est 1919
p: Kings, New York
d:
p:

4 Howard Joseph Staudt
b: 2 Dec 1919
p:
m:
p:
d: 26 May 1984
p: Davidson, Tennessee

9 Lillian Veronica McGrath
b: abt 1901
p:
d:
p:

2 Daniel Eric Staudt
b: 8 Sep 1949
p:
m: 14 Apr 1973
p:
d:
p:

10 Gustus Eric Swanson
b: abt 1878
p: Sweeden
m:
p:
d: 6 Jun 1969
p:

5 Gloria Elwayne Swanson
b: 10 Aug 1921
p:
d: 6 Aug 1992
p:

11 Ethel Ray Pursley
b: abt 1893
p: Virginia
d:
p:

1 Kellye Danielle Staudt
b: 21 May 1982
p: Nashville, Tenn.
m: 23 Jul 2005
p: Nashville, Tenn.
d:
p:

sp: **William Derry Johnson**

12 John Kellum Mann
b: 8 Aug 1891
p:
m:
p:
d: 20 Jul 1968
p:

6 Charley Robert Mann
b: 23 Jan 1920
p:
m:
p:
d: 10 Aug 1978
p:

13 Missouri Martin
b:
p:
d:
p:

3 Vonda Joan Mann
b: 14 Jan 1953
p:
d:
p:

14 Charlie McClain Davis
b: 1 Aug 1900
p:
m:
p:
d: 9 Jan 1958
p:

7 Thelma Beatrice Davis
b: 14 Jan 1926
p:
d: 9 Apr 1963
p:

15 Mattie Elizabeth Arnold
b: 30 Jul 1906
p:
d: 16 Jul 1999
p:

16
b:
d:

17
b:
d:

18
b:
d:

19
b:
d:

20
b:
d:

21
b:
d:

22
b:
d:

23 Willie Ann Pursley
b:
d:

24
b:
d:

25
b:
d:

26
b:
d:

27
b:
d:

28
b:
d:

29
b:
d:

30
b:
d:

31 Cora Arnold
b:
d:

32 _____
33 _____
34 _____
35 _____
36 _____
37 _____
38 _____
39 _____
40 _____
41 _____
42 _____
43 _____
44 _____
45 _____
46 _____
47 _____
48 _____
49 _____
50 _____
51 _____
52 _____
53 _____
54 _____
55 _____
56 _____
57 _____
58 _____
59 _____
60 _____
61 _____
62 _____
63 _____

Pedigree Chart - Mia Mckenzie Johnson

Chart no. _____
No. 1 on this chart is the same as no. _____ on chart no. _____

1 Mia Mckenzie Johnson
b: 17 Jan 2008
p: Nashville, Tenn
m:
p:
d:
p:

sp:

2 William Derry Johnson
b: 10 Feb 1980
p: Flowood, Mississippi
m: 23 Jul 2005
p: Nashville, Tenn.
d:
p:

3 Kellye Danielle Staudt
b: 21 May 1982
p: Nashville, Tenn.
d:
p:

4 Steven Winslow Johnson
b: 2 Sep 1952
p: Houston, Texas
m: 11 Aug 1972
p: Kentwood, Louisiana
d:
p:

5 Juanita Elaine Magee
b: 3 May 1953
p: Tylertown, Miss.
d:
p:

6 Daniel Eric Staudt
b: 8 Sep 1949
p:
m: 14 Apr 1973
p:
d:
p:

7 Vonda Joan Mann
b: 14 Jan 1953
p:
d:
p:

8 Arta Elmer Johnson
b: 6 Jul 1927
p: North Carolina
m:
p:
d: 27 Aug 2003
p: Johnson City, Tenn

9 Betty Jean Henderson
b: 16 Jul 1931
p:
d: 20 Oct 2008
p: Johnson City, Tenn.

10 Derry David Magee
b: 5 Jul 1934
p: New Orleans, Louisiana
m: 11 Oct 1952
p: Mt.Hermon, Louisiana
d:
p:

11 Gwendora Wilkes Magee
b: 1 Sep 1936
p: Mt. Hermon, La.
d:
p:

12 Howard Joseph Staudt
b: 2 Dec 1919
p:
m:
p:
d: 26 May 1984
p: Davidson, Tennessee

13 Gloria Elwayne Swanson
b: 10 Aug 1921
p:
d: 6 Aug 1992
p:

14 Charley Robert Mann
b: 23 Jan 1920
p:
m:
p:
d: 10 Aug 1978
p:

15 Thelma Beatrice Davis
b: 14 Jan 1926
p:
d: 9 Apr 1963
p:

16 Arta E. Johnson
b: abt 1878
d:

17 Ruth Bell Pipes
b: 25 Sep 1886
d: 1987

18 William Henderson Jr.
b: 18 Jun 1909
d: 31 Aug 1963

19 Viola Emma Moody
b: 21 Apr 1912
d: bet 30 Jun 1996 and Jan

20 Marvin Mangum Magee
b: 18 Jul 1908
d: 6 Jan 1971

21 Mary Alline Bridges
b: 22 Aug 1914
d: 16 Sep 1990

22 Earl Samuel Wilkes
b: 5 Feb 1912
d: 29 Jan 1994

23 Willie Marie Burch
b: 30 Jan 1915
d: 8 Jan 2002

24 Howard Louis Staudt
b: abt 1900
d:

25 Lillian Veronica McGrath
b: abt 1901
d:

26 Gustus Eric Swanson
b: abt 1878
d: 6 Jun 1969

27 Ethel Ray Pursley
b: abt 1893
d:

28 John Kellum Mann
b: 8 Aug 1891
d: 20 Jul 1968

29 Missouri Martin
b:
d:

30 Charlie McClain Davis
b: 1 Aug 1900
d: 9 Jan 1958

31 Mattie Elizabeth Arnold
b: 30 Jul 1906
d: 16 Jul 1999

32 James H. Johnson

33 Zilpha Almedia Johnson

34 Thomas Pipes

35 Martha Emmline Cottrell

36 William T Henderson Sr.

37 Lee Annie Pattillo

38 Alex John Moody

39 Trudell Emma Riddle

40 Derry David Magee

41 Zora Easterling

42 Cannon Wilson Bridges

43 Juanita Rivers Bankston

44 Lucion Wilkes

45 Lavanda Armentha Morris

46 Arthur Burch Senior

47 Mary Jemima Foil

48

49

50

51

52

53

54

55 Willie Ann Pursley

56

57

58

59

60

61

62

63 Cora Arnold

Pedigree Chart - William Chase Johnson

Chart no. _____
No. 1 on this chart is the same as no. _____ on chart no. _____

1 William Chase Johnson
b: 20 Dec 2010
p: Nashville, Tenn
m:
p:
d:
p:

sp:

2 William Derry Johnson
b: 10 Feb 1980
p: Flowood, Mississippi
m: 23 Jul 2005
p: Nashville, Tenn.
d:
p:

3 Kellye Danielle Staudt
b: 21 May 1982
p: Nashville, Tenn.
d:
p:

4 Steven Winslow Johnson
b: 2 Sep 1952
p: Houston, Texas
m: 11 Aug 1972
p: Kentwood, Louisiana
d:
p:

5 Juanita Elaine Magee
b: 3 May 1953
p: Tylertown, Miss.
d:
p:

6 Daniel Eric Staudt
b: 8 Sep 1949
p:
m: 14 Apr 1973
p:
d:
p:

7 Vonda Joan Mann
b: 14 Jan 1953
p:
d:
p:

8 Arta Elmer Johnson
b: 6 Jul 1927
p: North Carolina
m:
p:
d: 27 Aug 2003
p: Johnson City, Tenn

9 Betty Jean Henderson
b: 16 Jul 1931
p:
d: 20 Oct 2008
p: Johnson City, Tenn.

10 Derry David Magee
b: 5 Jul 1934
p: New Orleans, Louisiana
m: 11 Oct 1952
p: Mt.Hermon, Louisiana
d:
p:

11 Gwendora Wilkes Magee
b: 1 Sep 1936
p: Mt. Hermon, La.
d:
p:

12 Howard Josepth Staudt
b: 2 Dec 1919
p:
m:
p:
d: 26 May 1984
p: Davidson, Tennessee

13 Gloria Elwayne Swanson
b: 10 Aug 1921
p:
d: 6 Aug 1992
p:

14 Charley Robert Mann
b: 23 Jan 1920
p:
m:
p:
d: 10 Aug 1978
p:

15 Thelma Beatrice Davis
b: 14 Jan 1926
p:
d: 9 Apr 1963
p:

16 Arta E. Johnson
b: abt 1878
d:

17 Ruth Bell Pipes
b: 25 Sep 1886
d: 1987

18 William Henderson Jr.
b: 18 Jun 1909
d: 31 Aug 1963

19 Viola Emma Moody
b: 21 Apr 1912
d: bet 30 Jun 1996 and Jan

20 Marvin Mangum Magee
b: 18 Jul 1908
d: 6 Jan 1971

21 Mary Alline Bridges
b: 22 Aug 1914
d: 16 Sep 1990

22 Earl Samuel Wilkes
b: 5 Feb 1912
d: 29 Jan 1994

23 Willie Marie Burch
b: 30 Jan 1915
d: 8 Jan 2002

24 Howard Louis Staudt
b: abt 1900
d:

25 Lillian Veronica McGrath
b: abt 1901
d:

26 Gustus Eric Swanson
b: abt 1878
d: 6 Jun 1969

27 Ethel Ray Pursley
b: abt 1893
d:

28 John Kellum Mann
b: 8 Aug 1891
d: 20 Jul 1968

29 Missouri Martin
b:
d:

30 Charlie McClain Davis
b: 1 Aug 1900
d: 9 Jan 1958

31 Mattie Elizabeth Arnold
b: 30 Jul 1906
d: 16 Jul 1999

32 James H. Johnson

33 Zilpha Almedia Johnson

34 Thomas Pipes

35 Martha Emmline Cottrell

36 William T Henderson Sr.

37 Lee Annie Pattillo

38 Alex John Moody

39 Trudell Emma Riddle

40 Derry David Magee

41 Zora Easterling

42 Cannon Wilson Bridges

43 Juanita Rivers Bankston

44 Lucion Wilkes

45 Lavanda Armentha Morris

46 Arthur Burch Senior

47 Mary Jemima Foil

48

49

50

51

52

53

54

55 Willie Ann Pursley

56

57

58

59

60

61

62

63 Cora Arnold

D. Magee History by Leslie Magee, Jr.

MAGEE FAMILY HISTORY

This Magee Family History is taken in an abbreviated form from a Magee Family Tree researched by Leon Walker, Collins, MS (1895-1971) and from information furnished by other family members. It reflects decendents of Alpin, King of Scotland, directly to the great grand children of Willis and Mary Norwood Magee. It does not attempt to follow all branches of the Magee family.

Alpin, King of Scotland, ascended the Scottish throne in 787 A.D. and died in 834 A.D.. His third son, Prince Gregor had two sons of whom the eldest was Constantine who m Malvina, daughter of Donald VI, King of Scotland. His son,Gregor, m Dorbiggelda. He died about 961 in battle with the Danes. His eldest son, John, m Alpine, daughter of Angus. He died about 1004 and his son, Gregor, Laird of Glenurchy, fought under Duncan I against the Normans and Danes. Gregor m a daughter of Campbell of Lochnow. Gregor's son, Sir John Gregor m the daughter of Henry, Prince of Scotland. Sir John died in 1238. His son, Lord of MacGregor, m Marion Gilchrist. He died in 1300. His son, Malcolm, Lord of MacGregor, m Mary, daughter of Malise MacAlpin. Malcolm died in 1374. He had two sons: One was Gregor, Lord MacGregor, his heir and successor, from whom is descended our line of Magees. Gregor, Lord MacGregor son of Malcolm, m Iris MacAlpin, daughter of Malcolm MacAlpin. He died in 1413. His son, John MacGregor first m a MacLaughlin, second a Macintosh, and third Helen Campbell. He died in 1461. By his first wife, the MacLaughlin, their second son, Gregor MacGregor, m Finvola (Flora) MacArthur of Strachur. Their son Duncan MacGregor m Mary, daughter of Lord Adkinlass. Their first son, Gregor MacGregor m Isabella Cameron, daughter of The Chieftain of Stornhead. Their son Duncan MacGregor was born in Lochabar. By his second m to a MacFarline, their first son was Patrick MacGregor, quite an outlaw in the Highlands in 1636. Patrick MacGregor m Marian MacLeod. Their second son James MacGregor (1645-1724) fought in his father's clan for the cause of King Charles I. As punishment for fighting with the losing side in this war, members of the MacGregor clan were ordered to change their names. James MacGregor changed his name to Thomas MacGehee. He came to Virginia in about 1650. Thomas MacGehee (formerly James MacGregor) m Ann Bastiop. Some members of his family later served with their relative Rob Roy MacGregor, famous Scottish outlaw who was sometimes called the "Robinhood of Scotland". James's son William (wife unknown) had a son William MacGehee Jr. (b 1722) who m Elizabeth McCulloch. Their son John MacGehee (b 1742) m Ann Moore. John and Ann Moore MacGehee had a son Phillip (1770-1826) who changed his name to Phillip Magee. The reason for change in spelling of his name is not known.

Phillip Magee (1770-1826) Son of John and Ann Moore MacGehee was born in Duplin County, North Carolina. He m Mary Butler (1773-1860) in North Carolina. They moved to what is now Simpson County and settled near present City of Magee. He was one of the areas earliest settlers. War of 1812 veteran. Their burial site is unknown. They had six children all born in North Carolina. 1. John (1791-1854) m Elizabeth Bowman. 2. Soloman (1795-1826) m Elizabeth Weathersby. 3. Catherine (1791-1852) m Henry Tolar. 4. Bersheba (1800-1876) m Richard Tullos and J. Gruber. 5. Elizabeth (1790-1826) m Woody Jones and James Lewis. 6. Robert (1793-1859) m Margaret Graves. He was one of the wealthiest men in county. Owned several thousand acres in Simpson and Covington Counties. Buried in Magee Cemetery located near old Jaynesville.

Soloman Magee (son of Phillip and Mary Butler Magee) and wife Elizabeth Weathersby had five children. 1. Catherine (b 1816) m Asa Walker. 2. Willis (1818-1883) m Mary Norwood (1817-1900). Served in the state legislature from Covington County, MS. Their burial site is unknown. 3. Mary Jane (1820-1821). 4. Sarah Adeline (1823-1904) m Buck Shivers. 5. Wilson (b 1825).

Willis Magee (son of Soloman and Elizabeth Magee) and wife Mary Norwood had nine children. They were:
1. Robert Soloman (1845-1888) m Eugenia Mangum. First Postmaster of Magee, MS. City of Magee named for him. Buried in Old Magee Cemetery. Children: (a) Derry David - (1866-1929) m Zora Easterling. Children: Galloway, Marvin Mangum and Ruth Annette. (b) Walter Lemuel - (b 1874). m Mattie Thames. Children: Marie. (c) John Mangum - (1881-1960) m a Baker. (d) Fannie - m John Smith. Children: Clifton, Guice, Vardaman and Gladys. (e) Lora T. - (1879-1963) m Ben Burkett. Children: Robert, Bessie, Jay and Maggie. (f) Margaret or Mattie - (b 1883) m a Brown. (g) Ella - m S. D. Doolittle. (h) Pearl - (1885-1964) m Leslie Walker and Claude Pope. (i) Willis Sims - (1878-1879). (j) Frances Lulda - (b 1868). (k) Mary - (b 1870) m a Tullos.
2. John N. (1843-1904) m Isabella Malloy. Both buried in the Malloy Cemetery. Children: (a) Owens Weathersby - (1874-1891). (b) Willis Archie - (1873-1925). (c) Euphemia - (1876-1960). (d) Sally J. - (1878-1952). (e) Mary C. - (1879-1928). (f) John Grenald - (1881-1967) m Emma Catherine Carr. Children: Carr, Lois, John Melvin and Marvin. (g) Robert Soloman - (1883-1948). m Ina Walker. Was Simpson County Supervisor for sixteen years. Children: John Hugh, Virgil Watkins, Mattie Hazel, Clifton Owen, Robert Soloman Jr. and Mary Inez. (h) Harriet Eugenia - (1887-1953). m a Valentine. (i) Duncan Malloy - (1885-1966) m Sarah Maddox. Children: Lavonne Nannie, Mildred Rea, John Duncan, Owens Alfred, Annie Bell, Ora Nell, Danial Allen, Paul Ernest, Euphemia Rebecca, Willis Eugene and Archie Malloy.
3. Owen Weathersby (1855-1931) m Ida Virginia Stamps. Both buried in the Mt. Zion Church Cemetery.
4. Margaret Louise (1840-1862) m John Covington. Children: Lora Covington. 5. Walter Lauren (1850-1904) m Melissa Tullos. 6. Harriet m a Hays. 7. Betty m a Grayson 8. Sarah C. (b 1841) m a Derryberry. 9. Elizabeth Carolyn (1848-1905) m a Floyd.

Compiled by: Leslie Magee Jr
Mendenhall, MS

180

E. Derry David Magee Obituary

Collins paper   Oct. 1929

D. D. Magee Passes to His Reward
Community Loses Most Valuable Citizen
Funeral Rites of our Beloved Brother Held Monday afternoon at 2:30 o'clock in the
Methodist Church

In the death of D. D. Magee, which occurred in his home Oct. 27, 1929 at 12:00 o'clock
Sunday night this community has lost one of its most valuable citizens, a Christian
gentleman of the highest type. The whole town, county and state mourn his passing
and deeply sympathize with his grief stricken family. Mr. Magee had been suffering
for some time and finding no relief - his family physician advised him to go away for
treatment which he did, but without avail, and a change for the worse soon came.

Mr. Magee was born May 20, 1866 in the historic old town of Magee and was the son
of Robert Solomon and Eugenia E. Magee. He was married to Miss Alice Thompson, March
11, 1894 and she was a noble christian character, but he did not have her but a few
short years until God called her home; later he married Miss Zora Easterling ; she
too was a strong character and a devoted wife and mother. To this union three
children were born, Charles Galloway, Ruth and Marvin and with this noble wife and
these dear children his home life was most pleasant; he was a devoted husband and a
loving father, a christian to the highest type, a wise counselor to his children, to
his family and to his community in which he lived. Right in the midst of his supreme
happiness with this dear good wife and children it was all broken by the death angel
carrying away the wife and mother, but this strong christian man struggled alone with
his children until March 5, 1922 when he married Miss Susie Elizabeth Smith, who has
been a devoted wife and a loving mother for them, who with the two sons, two grandchildren, Collins, Miss. and the one daughter, who is Mrs. Clyde Polk, Slidell, La.
survive him. He is also survived by four sisters and two brothers, W. L. Magee,
Collins; John M. Magee, Senatobia, Mrs. S. R. Doolittle and Mrs. J. D. Brown, Newton;
Mrs. B. B. Burkett, Hattiesburg, Mrs. W. L. Walker, Laurel . We shall miss the help
and guidance of his ever inspiring presence and the words of wisdom which he always
had to offer. We have felt that the thing that secured his stamp of approval was
worthy of due consideration because his judgment was ever the result of intelligent
and clear thinking.

Although Mr. Magee will walk with us no more the influence of his noble exemplary
life will always be felt in our town, county and state. He has been a member of
the Board of Stewards of Collins Methodist Church nearly thirty years and was a
steward in his church before he came to Collins. He served for years as a member of
the Board of Supervisors and at the time of his death was a member of the Board of
Alderman of Collins. He was by trade a brick and cement contractor and a pioneer
citizen to the city of Collins and we doubt if there can be found in Collins any
houses but that he has had to do with the construction thereof.

The funeral services were held at the Methodist Church on Monday afternoon at 2:30
o'clock, where an immense congregation gathered to pay a last tribute of love and
respect, many coming from distant towns and cities. The deluge of flowers spoke
eloquently of the esteem in which he was held. The funeral rites were conducted by
his pastor, Rev. P. H. Grice, assisted by Rev. J. T. Dale, Rev. W. B. Abel and Mr.
Blackwell, all paying a beautiful tribute to his life and character; there was no
particular text for this occasion but many suitable passages were read and poems
quoted as fitting the life that had just passed from us.

" A city that is set on a hill cannot be hid." "His was truly a life that shone
out above others." "Know ye not that there is a prince and a great man fallen
this day in Israel, and that this christian father was the greatest heritage we might
seek. These men of God also said when such a man is taken from us, we feel the force
of the prophet's words, when he said at the death of Abraham and also Isaac,
"Let me die the death of the righteous and let my last end be like his.

Our town has lost a great man, a good and useful man. The church has lost a consecrate
christian worker. Each of us have lost a friend and brother and his family has lost
a princely companion and father.

In this beautiful tribute many comforting words were said to the wife, children,
sisters, brothers, relatives and friends.

"May God enable us all like him to live so that when we come to die we may like him
die the death of the righteous. The husband and father, brother and friend, so
devoted and true, so watchful, so anxious, with love ever new - a friend so faithful
in sorrow and strife has ended his course, the rough pathway of life; weep not for
him he is happy on high, in yonder safe mansions; that home in the sky, his mission
is ended; his trials are past.

Following the service the body was in charge of undertaker, P. A. Johns and was
conveyed to Salem Cemetery for interment.

Active pallbearers were Mayor G. H. Merrell, Clerk F. C. McRaney, Marshall J. T.
Duckworth, Commissioners C. E. Vaughn and Alderman T. J. Thames, J. J. Beech and
J. W. Walker.

F. THE BURCH FAMILY

Richard Burch as born in Georgia about 1783. He settled three headrights in Washington Parish. One headright was in the Mt. Pisgah Community. He settled two headrights on Big Silver Creek. These two headrights adjoin one another. Louisiana Highway 38 crosses the lower one. Richard Burch moved to Mississippi. He was last reported alive in Rankin County in 1855.

One or more children of Richard Burch remained in Washington Parish. John R. Burch, Sr. was one of these children. He married Samantha Clowers, born April 22, 1810 and died December 1, 1891. She was a sister or close relative of A. J. Clowers who was an early member of the Spring Creek Masonic Lodge. John R. Burch, Sr. died between 1832-1836. He is believed to be buried in an unmarked grave hear his wife in the Burch Cemetery near Mt. Pisgah Baptist Church. Her grave is a brick tomb with a marble slab on top. (Note: We visited this Burch Cemetery in November, 2010 and found the brick tomb to be in need of repair and without any marble slab or any top on the tomb. There is an unmarked grave next to Samantha's tomb that has a sandstone at the foot. We were wondering if this were his grave.)

John R. Burch, Jr. was born on January 9, 1836 and died on January 15, 1914. He was the son of John R. Burch, Sr. and Samantha (Lewis) and evidently was left an indigent orphan upon his father's death. In the *History of Washington Parish* written by Hon. Prentiss B. Carter, we find, "The son of John R. Burch, Sr., who built the first storehouse in our little town, said son being John R. Jr., was one of the ten 'indigent orphans' to attend the first sessions of this school in 1838. This charter school, Franklinton Academy, was the first organized attempt towards a higher system of education in the parish. This school received a subsidy by the State of $1,000 a year for five years.

John R. Burch, Jr. was one of the pupils attending the Franklinton Academy when it constructed its first building on the Bogue Chitto River after the Legislature appropriated on March 28, 1840 an additional $1500.00 for its construction. Pupils came from surrounding parishes and Mississippi counties which indicated that there were no schools during these five or six years in these areas.

John R. Burch, Jr. was a student in the next school of formal organization in 1852. Assisted by the Peabody Fund and organized by the Bickhams and Magees, a "box-house" school was built at Half-Moon Bluff, which is near the present site of Clifton.

During John R. Burch, Jr.'s early life, he was an overseer on the Dr. William L. Magee Plantation. This was one of the largest pre-Civil War plantations in Washington Parish. There were 59 slaves on this plantation in 1860. He later was a mail carrier, and his later life he was a prosperous farmer in the Mt. Pisgah area.

John R. Burch, Jr. enlisted in the Washington Rifles when it was organized in Franklinton during June, 1861 by Capt. Hardy C. Richardson. This company was mustered into the Confederate Army at Camp Moore as Co. "I," 9th La. Infantry. John R. Burch, Jr. was wounded in the Battle of Sharpsburg, Md. on September 19, 1862. His wound disabled him for the rest of the war.

John R. Burch, Jr. was an active member of Franklinton Masoic Lodge 101 for sixty years. He was Worshipful Master of the Lodge in 1880. (See the Lodge's account of John's service to his country and to the Lodge 101 written by Daunton Gibbs, P.M., Lodge 101, F.&A.M., Franklinton, LA., 1957.)

John R. Burch, Jr. married Melissa Brumfield on April 24, 1863. She was born Oct. 22, 1843 and died on June 7, 1923. Melissa was a daughter of John W. Brumfield and granddaughter of Ezekiel Brumfield who died at Camp Morgan (near Madisonville) during the Battle of New Orleans Campaign in the

184

winter of 1814-1815. She was a granddaughter of John Brumfield, Sr., a Revolutionary War Veteran who settled in Washington Parish. John and Melissa had 12 children.

John R. Burch, Jr. was a half brother of Abner C. Bickham and Edward Myles.

Daunton Gibbs, 1977
Burch Data
Hon. Prentiss Carter's
"History of Washington Parish"

G. JOHN R. BURCH
TYLER, LODGE 101, F.& A.M., FRANKLINTON, LOUISIANA

Bro. John R. Burch was born January 9, 1832. He was the son of John Burch, Sr. who lived in the Mt. Pisgah Community and who was listed in Judge Carter's History of Washington Parish as one of the early students of the old Franklinton Academy, first school established in Franklinton. His grandfather was Richard Burch who came from Germany and settled the Richard Burch headrights in the Mt. Pisgah Community shortly after 1800. His mother was Symanthia (Samantha) Clowers who married five times before her death and who had children by three of her five husbands. She is believed to have been a close relative, perhaps a brother of Bro. A. J. Clowers (made a Master Mason in 1864).

Symanthia (Samantha) Clowers first married a Lewis and after his death married John Burch, Sr., father of Bro. John R. Burch. (Correction made by Gwendora Wilkes Magee – According to records in the *Southern Bickhams* and other family records, Samantha married John Burch, Sr. first.) After the death of John Burch, Sr., she married Thomas Bickham, son of Capt. Abner Bickham, Sr., who settled in Washington Parish about 1807. After the death of Thomas Bickham, she married Dr. Myles who came from Ireland and practiced medicine in the Mt. Pisgah community. Dr. Myles died and she then married a Holmes from whom she separated. Her fifth and last marriage was to William Lewis. This unusual series of marriages made Bro. John R. Burch a half-brother to Bro. Abner C. Bickham and to Bro. Edward Myles.

Bro. John R. Burch married Melissa Brumfield, daughter of Jack Brumfield, and established his home in the Mt. Pisgah Community where he lived all of his life. The 1850 census of Washington Parish has him listed as a Mail Carrier. Several years before the outbreak of the Civil War he became an overseer on the plantation of Dr. William L. Magee. This was the largest plantation in the Mt. Pisgah section. In 1860 there were 58 slaves on this plantation. The home of Dr. William L. Magee was near the present home of Frank Bahm.

On July 7, 1861, Bro. Burch enlisted in the Washington Rifles, being organized at the time in Franklinton by Bro. Hardy C. Richardson, who became its first commanding officer. The company then moved to the Half-Moon Bluff Baptist Church where it camped and trained for two weeks. This site is on Bogue Chitto River just back of the Ferd Magee place on the Clifton Highway. From Half-Moon Bluff Church, the company moved to Camp Moore in Tangipahoa Parish on the New Orleans, Jackson and Great Northern Railroad (now Illinois Central). In Camp Moore, the Washington Rifles was reassigned as Co. "I" of the Ninth La. Infantry, but remained intact as far as the company officers and men were concerned. Command of the Ninth La. Infantry had been assigned to Col. Richard Taylor, brilliant soldier-son of Gen. Zachary Taylor, Louisiana's first and only President. Col. Taylor was a Yale University graduate and a wealthy St. Charles Parish plantation owner.

The Ninth La. Infantry's stay as Camp Moore was short because the Federal Army was already about to Launch its first assault against the Confederate Capitol of Richmond which was to be climaxed by the First Battle of Manassas. Col. Taylor immediately turned command of the Regiment over to his second-in-command, Lt. Col. Randolph, while he went to New Orleans in an effort to obtain equipment and supplies for his men. The Regiment entrained for Virginia in an effort to reach there before the first assault on Richmond. The route was north over the New Orleans, Jackson and Great Northern Railroad into Tennessee, and from there over to Virginia. However, due to a faulty locomotive on the last stage of the trip, the troops failed to reach Manassas in time for the battle. The locomotive was so weak, the troops were forced to dismount from the train and assist the locomotive in pushing the empty cars over some of the hills. They reached Manassas Junction at dusk on the final day of the battle which resulted in the Federal Army being defeated.

Col. Taylor was promoted to General in October, 1861 and moved his troops, including the Ninth La. Infantry, to Camp Carondelet, Va., where he set up a program of intensive training. This program brought the troops to a high state of efficiency and discipline which was to seen pay off because in the early Spring of 1862, Gen. Taylor, his Louisiana troops were able to perform some great feats of marching and maneuvering. As a result, Gen. Taylor became one of Stonewall Jackson's most trusted generals, and the fame of Stonewall Jackson, himself, rose to excel that of all Confederate Generals except Gen. Robert E. Lee, the commander-in-chief.

Gen. Taylor and his Louisiana troops, including the Washington Rifles, was in one campaign after another, each taking a toll of local men, dead, wounded and captured. The Second Battle of Manassas, fought in September of 1862, was perhaps the worst up until that time.

Bro. John R. Burch was severely wounded in the desperate fighting around Fredericksburg, Md. in late 1862. He was discharged as a result of his wounds in early 1863, and returned home.

Bro. Burch took over his old position as an overseer on the Dr. William L. Magee Plantation. However, a young Dr. William L. Magee had died in 1861, and the plantation was now in the hands of his widow, and her second husband, Capt. Wiley G. Collins. Capt. Collins was a Confederate Army Captain, discharged because of wounds.

This large plantation, stripped of most if its slaves, and other ravages of War, soon broke up. As a result, Bro. Burch was soon farming his own place. He became one of the most prominent farmers and citizens in his community. He was Treasurer of Washington Parish for a number of years.

Bro. Burch was made a Master Mason in Lodge 101, Franklinton, La. in 1954. He served the Lodge as Tyler in 1856; Junior Deacon in 1861; Senior Deacon in 1964 and 1965; Senior Warden in 1871, 1873, 1878, and 1879. He served the Lodge as Worshipful Master in 1880. He was Treasurer of the Lodge in 1886, 1887, and 1888.

Bro. Burch died at his home on June 15, 1914. He was buried in the family Cemetery near Mt. Pisgah Baptist Church. Masonic services were conducted by Judge Prentis B. Carter. Bro. Burch rendered the Lodge long and faithful service. At the time of his death, he had been a member of Lodge 101 sixty years. He was the father of Bro. Weston Burch. Among his grandsons who are members of Lodge 101, are Bros. John P., Frank and Lamar Richardson.

Daunton Gibbs, P. M., Lodge 101, F. & A. M., Franklinton, La., 1957

*The following information was taken from *The Southern Bickhams* by John Dorr Crane, published in 1994. Samantha Clowers' first marriage was to John Richard, Sr. After his death in 1832-1836, his wife Samantha married Thomas Bickham (1795-1838). Thomas was the fourth child of Abner Bickham (1755-1834) I quote from the Crane's book:

"The fourth child of Abner was referred to as 'Thomas Bickham, Jr.' when he was appointed by his mother as her attorney-in-fact in 1834. Presumably, Thomas Sr. would have been his uncle. There are other instances in that time of nephews who had the same name as an uncle being called 'Junior,' e.g., William, son of John."

"Thomas died in about 1838 in Washington Parish. He apparently lived in St. Helena Parish, as the parish judge of Washington Parish directed the parish judge of St. Helena Parish to inventory the 'property of Thomas Bickham of St. Helena Parish."

"His wife Samantha, had previously been married to John Burch, Sr. and had two children by him (John R. Burch, Jr. and ?Nancy Burch). She and Thomas also had two children (Abner Clower Bickham and ?). After Thomas' death she married Isaac A. Myles, and they had at least two children (Edward Myles and Rebecca Myles). The name of her fourth husband was Coleman Holmes (whom she divorced). She married her fifth and last, William Lewis, in 1860. She outlived her last husband by 14 years; he died in 1874, she in 1891 at age 80."

Note: William Lewis was Samantha's fifth and last husband which could explain why her tombstone in the Burch Cemetery reads, "Samantha Lewis." She was born on April 22, 1810 and died December 1, 1891." This could also explain why a grave marker was never placed on John Richard Burch, Sr.'s grave. Records indicate that John was buried in the Burch Cemetery in an unmarked grave near Samantha's brick tomb and marker. There is a large sandstone at the foot of an unmarked grave next to her tomb. Could this be John Richard Burch, Sr.'s grave? Or could this grave next to Samantha be her son's, Abner Clower Bickham (10-19-1836-1-26-1911) buried there according to the Burch Cemetery records.

H. JUANITA RIVERS BRIDGES

Juanita Rivers Bankston Bridges was born in Grangeville, Louisiana in St. Helena Parish on July 15, 1885 and died on October 5, 1965. She married Cannon Wilson Bridges on March 6, 1906. He was born in St. Helena Parish, Louisiana on March 22, 1848 and died in St. Helena Parish, Louisiana in December, 1923. Juanita and Cannon had three children: Iddo Lampton Bridges, Susie Elizabeth Jenkins, and Mary Alline Magee. Juanita, my maternal grandmother, was a very special woman in my life and in the lives of

Juanita and Cannon Brideges

my wife Dora and daughter, Juanita Elaine Magee. I had so much love and respect for her that Gwendora and I named our only child and daughter, Juanita Elaine Magee, after her.

While I was attending college at LSU and at TAMU, Grandmother Bridges sent me five dollars every month. This might not sound like a lot of money but coming out of her meager old age pension (less than $100.00 a month), it was a large gift over the six years of my attending college.

Grandmother was always there when we made the 13 moves during the time that I was a student at LSU and TAMU. After Dora's surgery in 1955, Dora and Nita returned to College Station, TX to join me in a two bedroom house on the front end of Cooner Street that I had rented from Dr. Jones. In preparation for Dora and Nita's return to College Station, Grandma came and stayed with Dora at the farm helping her prepare for the move back to Texas. While there Grandma helped Dora refinish an oak dresser that Dora's parents had given her. The dresser had been a wedding present to Earl and Willie Wilkes from Willie's parents. It turned out that there was not enough room in the truck to bring the dresser to College Station; therefore, it was returned to the

Wilkes house where it remained until the household items were distributed to the Wilkes children.

Grandmother Bridges had a tough life. She married Cannon Bridges, who had been married approximately six times and was much older than she. Cannon was 54 years old and Juanita was 19 years old when they married on March 6, 1906. He was very abusive to her and their three children, Iddo, Susie, and Mary Bridges.

On one occasion, Cannon beat Juanita causing her and the children to flee to Zack Travis's house at Gillsburg, Mississippi for a safe place. In order for Iddo to help protect his mother, he carried a gun just in case his father tried to kill them. Grandma had Cannon committed to a hospital for the criminally insane in Jackson, Louisiana. The Travis family later got him out of the facility.

Juanita's daughter Mary, my mother, had nightmares throughout her life fearing that her father Cannon would come and kill them. In fact, a short time before her death, she walked over to her daughter Mary Jane's house very disheveled. Mary Jane asked her what was wrong. Mary replied, "I dreamed that Papa chased us all night."

Grandmother Juanita did not have a home to call her own but primarily lived with her daughter, Susie Bridges Jenkins in the Ponchatoula, La. area. She spent time visiting her son Iddo Bridges in New Orleans and my mother, Mary Magee, who lived in several locations in Tangipahoa and Livingston Parishes as a pastor's wife. Her life was dedicated to taking care of family and friends.

Mary, Marvin and Juanita

Grandma Bridges, Aunt Susie, and my mother, Mary moved to Baton Rouge, La. where Grandma worked at an orphanage for females to provide a safe shelter for her and her daughters. Her son, Iddo Bridges, stayed with his grandfather, Thomas Jefferson Bankston in Grangeville, La., which was located in St. Helena Parish. With a strong desire to get her family back together, Grandma asked "Big Sis" Knight who taught school in Bogalusa, La. to find her a job in the Bogalusa area. Grandma and the three children rode the train from Baton Rouge via Slidell to Bogalusa. She got a job at a plant nursery and one grandchild recalls that she worked plowing a mule on a Tung Oil farm in the Folsom, La. area.

While living in Bogalusa, Grandmother's daughter Susie met Joe Jenkins, and with Grandma's permission she married him at the age of 13. At some point, Iddo went to New Orleans, lied about his age (about 16 at that time) and got a job working for the New Orleans Public Service Department where he worked in various positions until he retired. Grandmother and daughter Mary went to New Orleans to live with Iddo where Mary attended and graduated high school while Grandma kept house for the family. While attending school in New Orleans, my mother met my father, Marvin Mangum Magee. Marvin and Iddo worked together for the City with Marvin working as a streetcar conductor.

My mother was dating my dad's friend Booker, but when Daddy saw Mother, he told Booker that it was now every man for himself. Daddy even used Booker's car to date Mother. Basically, Booker was pushed out of the picture by my father. Mother and Daddy married on October 25, 1931 in Collins, Miss.

On one occasion, mother went on a trip with daddy, and Grandmother Juanita Bankston Bridges came to stay with my sister Jane and me. Jane was a trouble maker and was doing something that grandmother told her to quit doing. I piped up and told Jane that she did not have to listen to that old woman. What a mistake! Grandmother grabbed me and really straightened out my attitude and comprehension. And then she got Jane. I do not want to give the wrong impression of her because she was very kind and considerate. Whenever any of her family needed help with moving or help with the arrival of a new baby or help of any kind, she was always present. However, she did not tolerate misbehavior from any of her grandchildren.

After I married and was a student at LSU, Grandmother came to our present home for a week to get us packed and traveled to our next home to unpack us. She was an excellent cook and was allowed to take over the kitchen whenever she was in our home. We moved 13 times while I was a student at LSU for two years and four years at Texas A & M. We always moved back to Louisiana to help on the farm or to work at some other summer job available. After Dora began working, we remained in College Station for the last two years before my graduation on May, 1958.

When Dora drove our daughter Juanita (Nita) to the orthodontist on Saturday from Kentwood, La. to New Orleans, they always stopped in Ponchatoula on their way back from New Orleans for a visit with Grandmother at Aunt Susie Jenkins. Grandmother was "Grandma" to Dora and "Big Mamou" to Nita. Nita recalls how much she enjoyed raw oatmeal and milk which was always the usual snack for her at Aunt Susie's. To get to the outside toilet, Nita remembers crossing a little bridge which was built over the ditch that carried the water from the "artesian flow well."

Grandmother Juanita's life was dedicated to taking care of family and friends who were ill, recovering from surgery, or expecting a baby. She believed that each new mother should have help six weeks after the birth of the baby. While she spent time with her children, she also spent time with her sister Aunt Kate and her father at Grangeville. She never considered herself a guest in a home, but she believed that she was there for a purpose. She was there to help the family in many ways. Her mode of transportation was the Greyhound bus which allowed her to travel on her own to the homes where she was needed.

Grandmother and Aunt Susie cut and sewed fabric pieces together designing quilt tops which they quilted into beautiful covers for beds. They made each child, grandchild, and great-grandchild a quilt. My quilt was the "Star Quilt" with a purple backing, and our daughter's quilt was a Patch Quilt made up of fabric from some of her dress scraps with a red flannel backing. They used remnants from fabrics Aunt Susie had used in designing and making clothing for her family. People gave Grandmother wool pockets from worn out shirts. She cut and pieced the squares of wool to make a backing for a quilt. She made her mattress of cotton which was the usual bedding of her day.

Aunt Susie's husband Joe worked all his life at the cypress mill in Ponchatoula where he was able to get cypress lumber to build Grandmother a cabin on their property. The cabin had a roof made of

Juanita Rivers Bankston Brideges—Grangevile Cemetery

sheets of tin that were attached by nails on top of the tin. These nails left a small crack which allowed some rain to penetrate the roof. Grandma used a ladder to climb on the roof to stuff cloth in these small openings to keep out the rain, cold, and bugs. She moved all of her belongings that she had brought from her father's home at Grangeville into the one room cabin. Her belongings had been stored at Joe and Susie's house. The cabin provided a great place to set up the quilting frames for their quilting.

Grandmother believed that one should work just a few hours at the time on any time-consuming project. She felt that moving on to another chore was restful. She worked a few hours on the roof while the weather was cool and then moved onto quilting, dressmaking, or canning to finish out a day's work.

February 14, 2013

I. CANNON WILSON BRIDGES

My maternal grandfather, Cannon Wilson Bridges was born on March 22, 1848 (1851) in St. Helena Parish, Louisiana. He died in December, 1923 in New Orleans, Louisiana and was buried in the Jackson Cemetery, St. Helena Parish, Louisiana. Records indicate that he married seven times with his last marriage being to my maternal grandmother Juanita Rivers Bankston in 1906. They had three children: Iddo Lampton Bridges (1907-1980), Susie Elizabeth Jenkins (1911-1995), and Mary Alline Magee (1914-1990). My mother Mary Alline and my father Marvin Mangum Magee married on October 25, 1931 in Collins, Mississippi. They had three children: Derry David Magee, Marvin Mangum Magee (infant death) and Mary Jane Magee Fabre.

Juanita was 21 years of age and Cannon was 58

Jackson Cemetery St. Helena Parish, LA

years old when they married which made a 37 years-difference in their ages. Due to Cannon's abuse to Juanita, she and her children fled to a Travis home for safety. She had Cannon committed to the Mental Hospital in Jackson, La. where he was later removed from the facility by the Travis family. His wife Juanita and her children went to Grangeville, La. to live with her father until she could make arrangements to move to Baton Rouge, La. where she worked at a children's home for girls so that her daughters could live there and attend school. Her son Iddo remained with Grandpaw Bankston in Grangeville, La. until Juanita found a place to live and work in the Bogalusa, La. area where she could have all three children living with her.

Due to the failure of Juanita and Cannon's marriage, our family never learned any positive things about our grandfather Cannon. Dr. Charles Hubert Bridges, a grandson of Evelyn Lavinia Wilson and Cannon Wilson Bridges, conducted some research and found the following accounts of Cannon which provide us all with some information and positive history of our grandfather.

Dr. Bridges writes the following: "In 1879 before his marriage to Evelyn Lavinia Wilson, her mother wrote to an acquaintance in St. Helena Parish, Reverend Thomas W. Day, asking his opinion of Cannon as a man. His response was that Cannon had a bad reputation with the women. He stated that if Cannon did not behave, he would come to Leesville and personally hang him to a tree limb. She also wrote to S. H. Pearson at the Norvilla Collegiate Institute located at Greensburg, St. Helena Parish. He responded that he thought that Cannon was an honorable man who was having some problems for which he was not responsible but that he should be able to solve those. Cannon had married Dorothy Dillon and later found that she was pregnant with child that was conceived before the marriage. He requested and received a divorce. "

"Cannon and Evelyn subsequently had eight children, the last born about 1899. They were: Horace Henry Bridges (1880-1960), William Lee Bridges (1884-), Florence Bridges (1886-1942), Ola Mae Bridges (1888-1964), Eula Virginia Bridges (1892-1961), Andrew Rogenmore Bridges (1895-1970), Charles Maurice Bridges (1897-1968), and Bessie Ruth Bridges (1899-1976). Family history reports that he "ran off and left her." He then moved to St. Helena again and in 1906 married Juanita Rivers Bankston. Other marriages were to Serena Watson, one for which a name is not available and to Molly Wills. Among contemporary (1999) cousins in St. Helena Parish, he is referred to as our "marrying cousin.""

"After Cannon and Evelyn married, they moved from Greensburg, Louisiana where their first son Horace was born. With the coming of the railroad to Leesville, La., they moved there and built a boarding house and a saloon to serve the railroad employees. Cannon at one time, evidently about the time of their divorce, was a traveling salesman, there being one letter dated in December 1900 telling of his travails, especially the loss of his coat and how he suffered from the cold. Charles M. Bridges, on his discharge papers from the US Army stated that his father was a swamper on the railroad. One story printed in the Greensburg paper, along with a picture of him and Juanita Bankston Bridges, comments on his history as a memorable teacher in Greensburg schools. Although the story about his operating a saloon is well known, a photo of the building where he lived and worked at that time carried signs of "Café" and "Restaurant." Two other children were born in Leesville. "

"Family history has Cannon at one time Mayor of Provencal, La. and at other times as a constable there. In his later years, his wife Juanita had him committed to a mental institution from which he was later released upon the request of one of his sons by that marriage. " (Note: perhaps the request was made by a son from another marriage. He and Juanita only had one son, Iddo Lampton Bridges, who had to carry a gun to protect Juanita and the children from Cannon).

"One wonders? One family story has Evelyn running Cannon off and taking over the business herself. She is reported to have broken his hand with a stick of stove wood because of his teasing her. It is probable that he was named Cannon after an uncle Cannon Travis born 1788. He was married to Evelyn Lavinia WILSON in 1879 in Leesville, Louisiana. He was divorced from Evelyn Lavinia WILSON in 1902 in Leesville, Louisiana."

Dr. Charles M. Bridges and his wife Mildred Kruse from Brenham, TX live in College Station, TX. where Dr. Bridges served as Professor and Head, Department of Veterinary Pathology, College of Veterinary Medicine, Texas A&M University 1960-78; Retired Professor Emeritus, TAMU and TAES, College Station, TX 1986; and Adjunct Professor of Pathology, Baylor College of Medicine, Houston, TX 1978-95.

After Charles retired, he and Mildred became very focused on researching their family genealogies. They traveled many places which included St. Helena Parish where Charles began learning about his Bridges ancestors. They met a cousin Inez Bridges Tate, a local historian in the area, who gave them information on the Bridges. As Inez was talking to Charles, she stated, "Charles, you have a first cousin on the faculty at the LAMS at Texas A&M University, Dr. Derry Magee." Upon Charles' return to College Station, he went over to Derry's office to meet him. This began a very special relationship between these two cousins who were veterinarians and had taught for years at TAMU College of Veterinary Medicine just a building across from each other and had never met. Dora and I have enjoyed some special social times with Charles and Mildred in their home and in ours. We remain in close contact via telephone, e-mail, or just dropping off a fig loaf that they enjoy.

Dr. Bridges has researched and written accurate accounts of Bridges and Kruse genealogies for his children and has shared this history with us. We appreciate this gift of genealogy research that he has given to us. He has provided us with a great lineage of the Bridges ancestors traced back to the 30th generation in Lancashire, England.

February 14, 2013

Professional Addendums

A DIFFERENT KIND OF CAMPUS

"In the fall of 1997, two students were on their way to prison. But unlike most that have made the trip, they hadn't been convicted of crime." These students were seniors at Texas A&M College of Veterinary Medicine and chose this prison rotation because they knew that they would get to do a lot of different things. At one of the units of the Texas Department of Criminal Justice (TDCJ) students might vaccinate dogs, suture a wire cut on a cow, or consult on breeding goals for huge, purebred Landrace hogs.

Students enrolled in the veterinary program at Texas A&M University learn by practicing medicine alongside faculty veterinarians during their fourth and final years. While certain courses of study such as surgery and clinical practice are required, others are electives. About two-thirds of the students sign up for what is commonly referred to as the "prison rotation," spending two weeks on various TDCJ farms. Students who choose the prison rotation are not the only ones who benefit from the relationship between Texas A&M and TDCJ. Students on theriogenology (reproduction) and field service rotations do pregnancy checking, participate in the brucellosis control program, and worm and vaccinate horses. But students on the prison rotation get to try their skills at whatever comes along, gaining experience in any number of different situations.

On this particular Monday, the students were in their second week of the two-week rotation. They spent most of the day with Dr. Derry Magee at the Ellis and Estelle Units near Huntsville. About two o'clock, they headed south to Sugar Land, Texas where they stayed through Thursday working under the supervision of Dr. Charles Page. Then it was back north with Dr. Magee for the last day.

Magee and Page are two of the Texas A&M large animal faculty members whose instruction takes place on the 17 farm units of the Texas prison system. The veterinarian involved in the Texas A&M-TDCJ interagency agreement was Dr. Mark Young. As staff veterinarian, Young was responsible for overall management of the veterinary programs of TDCJ throughout

Texas. After Dr. Young retired, Dr. Magee assumed this responsibility.

About an hour and a half after leaving College Station, Magee and his students drove through the gates at the Ellis Unit. It's 7:30 a.m. A long line of wagons, each holding 16 inmates in white coveralls, waits to take the men to the fields. Guards on horseback stand ready. Frenzied barking cut the early morning stillness as hounds flung themselves against a kennel's chair link barrier. The dogs, bred and trained on each unit, filled the air with deep, continuous baying. A pack of ten accompanied every crew of prisoners that went out to work row crops such as cotton, maize, corn, hay, and vegetables. As the students watched, a signal was given, and the wagons began to move.

Confirming what the students had heard regarding the rotation, Magee said, "You don't ever know what you're going to do when you get there." He was proven right before he and the students left the truck. Instead of heading directly for the cattle awaiting them, the livestock supervisor directed them to the stables. A mare had cut her head badly in a collision with a post. It was a deep, jagged laceration that came dangerously close to the left eye. An inmate held the horse while the students examined the cut. At Magee's instruction, a student tranquilized the patient. After about 15 minutes, the horse's head hung low and the eyes were glazed, obvious effects of the medication. The students cleaned the wound and, as inmates and guards watched closely, a student sutured his first patient. When the job was finished, Magee gave the supervisor and one of the inmates instructions about care. The doctor and his students headed for the cattle pens.

Palpating cattle is hard, dirty work. The students stated that their primary reason for choosing the prison rotation was "to learn how to palpate cattle." The two students felt particularly fortunate because their rotation happened to fall during the season when pregnancy testing was at its height. On that morning, 137 cows were waiting.

Inmates moved the cattle through a round pen and into a squeeze chute. The inmates who handle cattle and maintain other livestock are trustees who are chosen based on past experience and interest. Trustees, unlike other Texas prison inmates, must work. They are "paid" in good-time credits. One of the students learned that one had been a trustee for 23 years.

The students changed places every ten cows; one palpated and, if the cow were pregnant, the other student, aided by inmates and an assistant livestock supervisor, drew blood for brucellosis certification, gave vaccinations and oral medication for internal parasites. Cows that were not pregnant were to be sold.

Dr. Magee concentrated as the students examined each squalling animal; he listed for the assessment-"pregnant" or, indicated a barren cow, "open." Then Dr. Magee palpated the cow himself to verify the finding. Under a tin-roofed shed next to the chute, the farm office manager recorded information as it was called out above the noise of bawling cattle. "7543." You said 7543?" "7543." "Work her."

Veterinary work is not for everyone. By two o'clock, the students were covered with feces, saliva, and milky-white worm medication. Their arms ached from being squeezed with the strong muscles of 137 cows. Their backs hurt from bending to reach the correct vein in the neck of a constantly moving cow. But these students were not unhappy. On a prison farm in East Texas, they were finally becoming veterinarians. They cleaned up a little, got in their truck, and headed for Dr. Page and the prison farms of South Texas.